Relaxing Wine Coloring Book

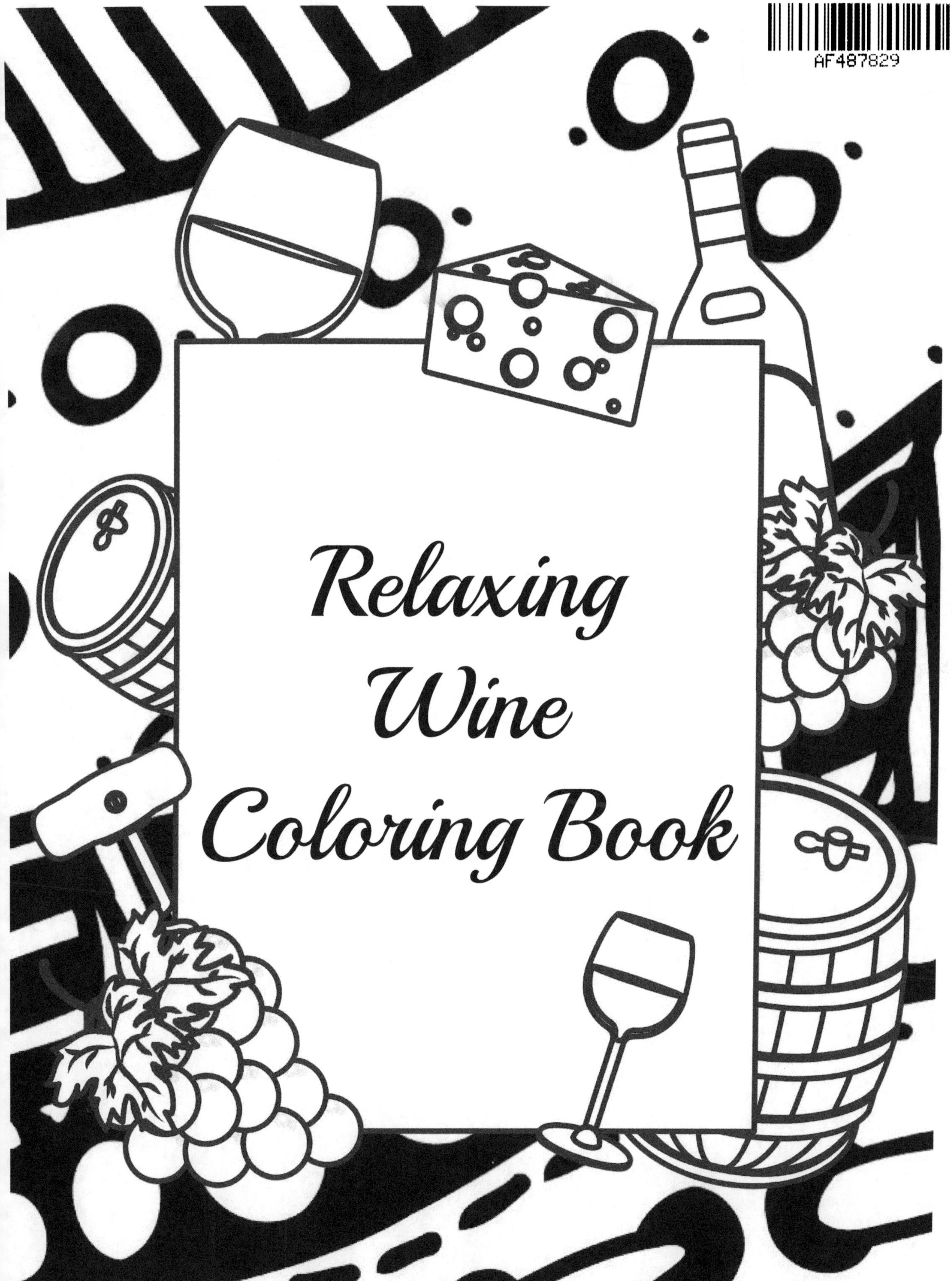

AF487829

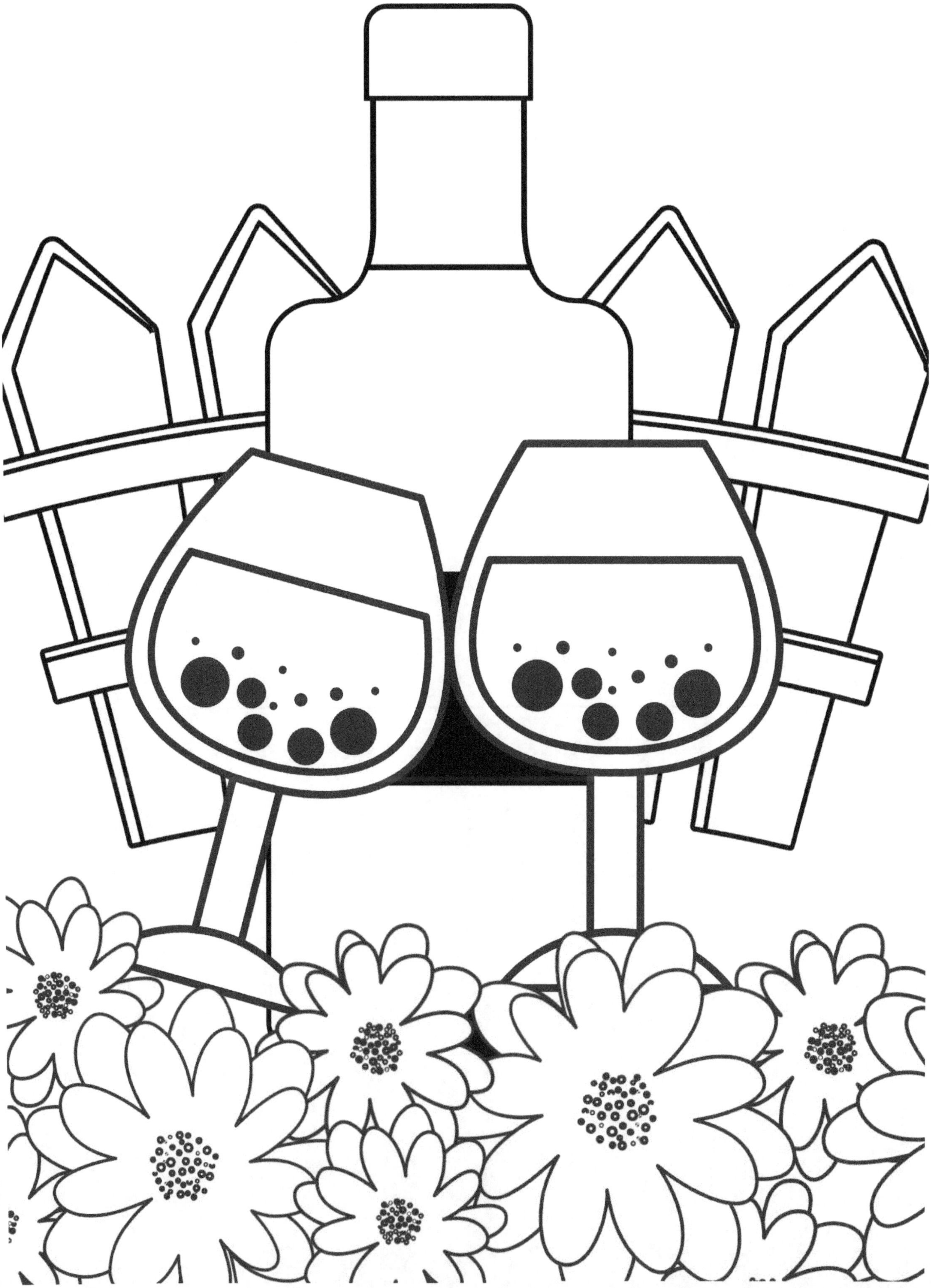

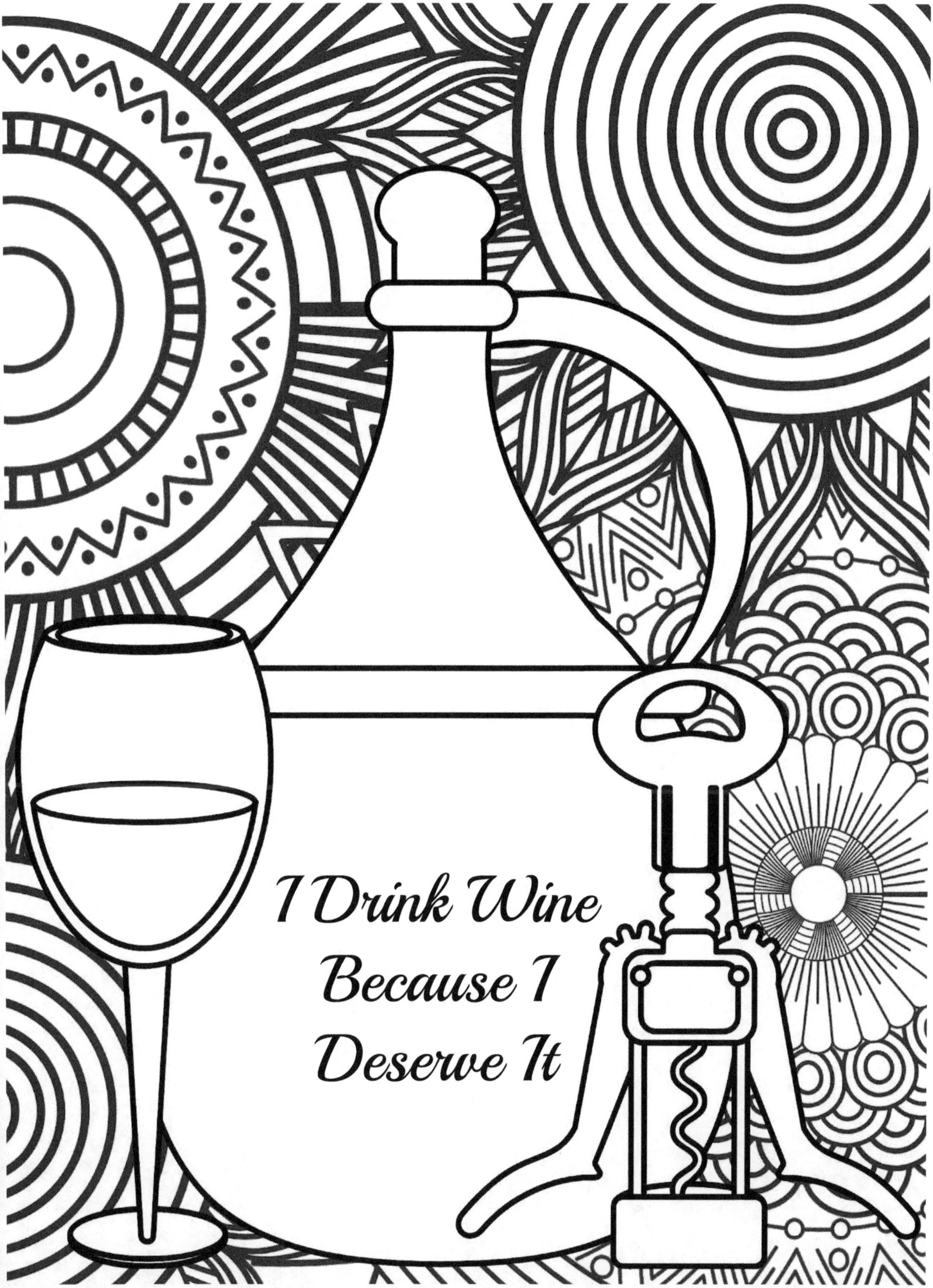
I Drink Wine
Because I
Deserve It

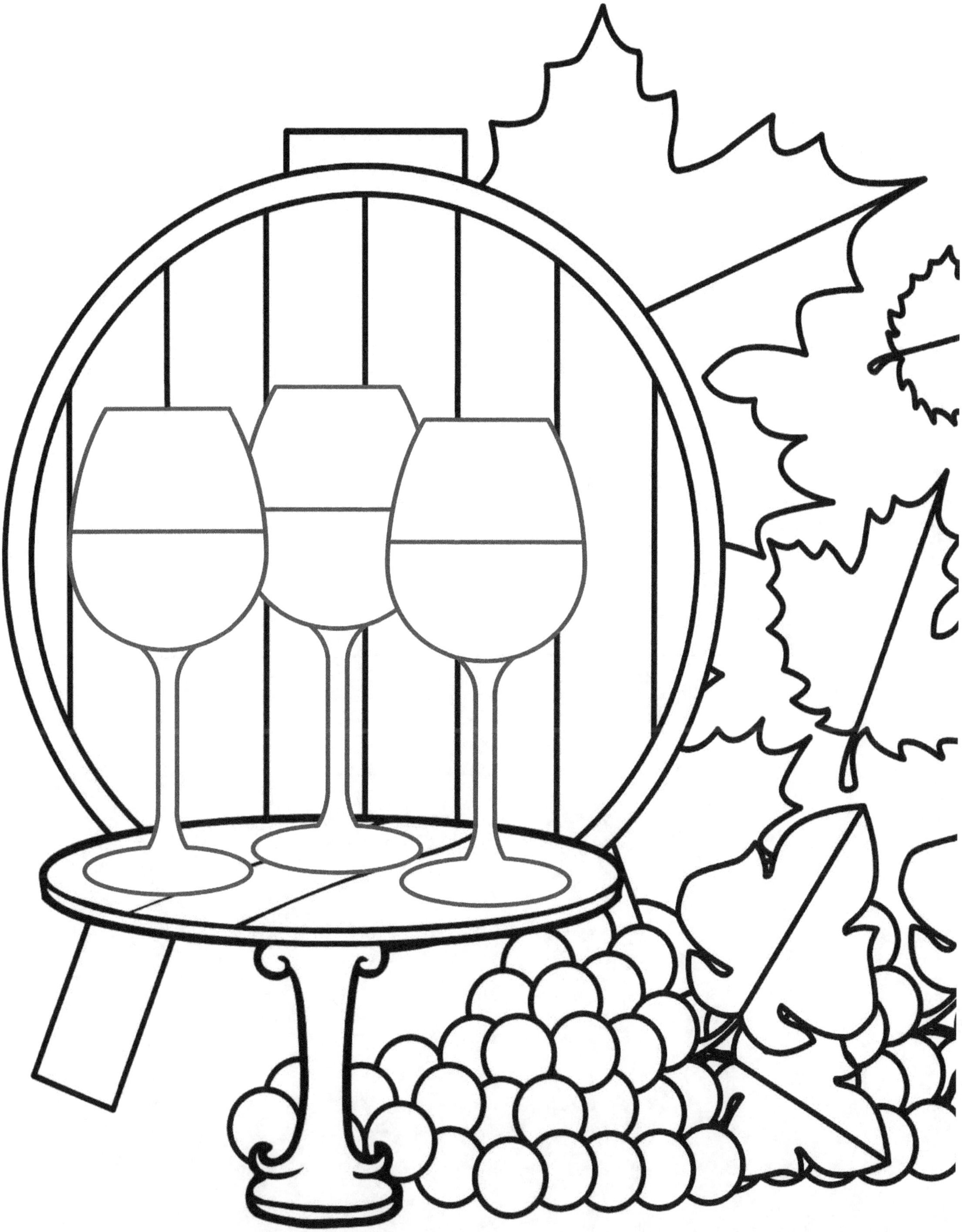

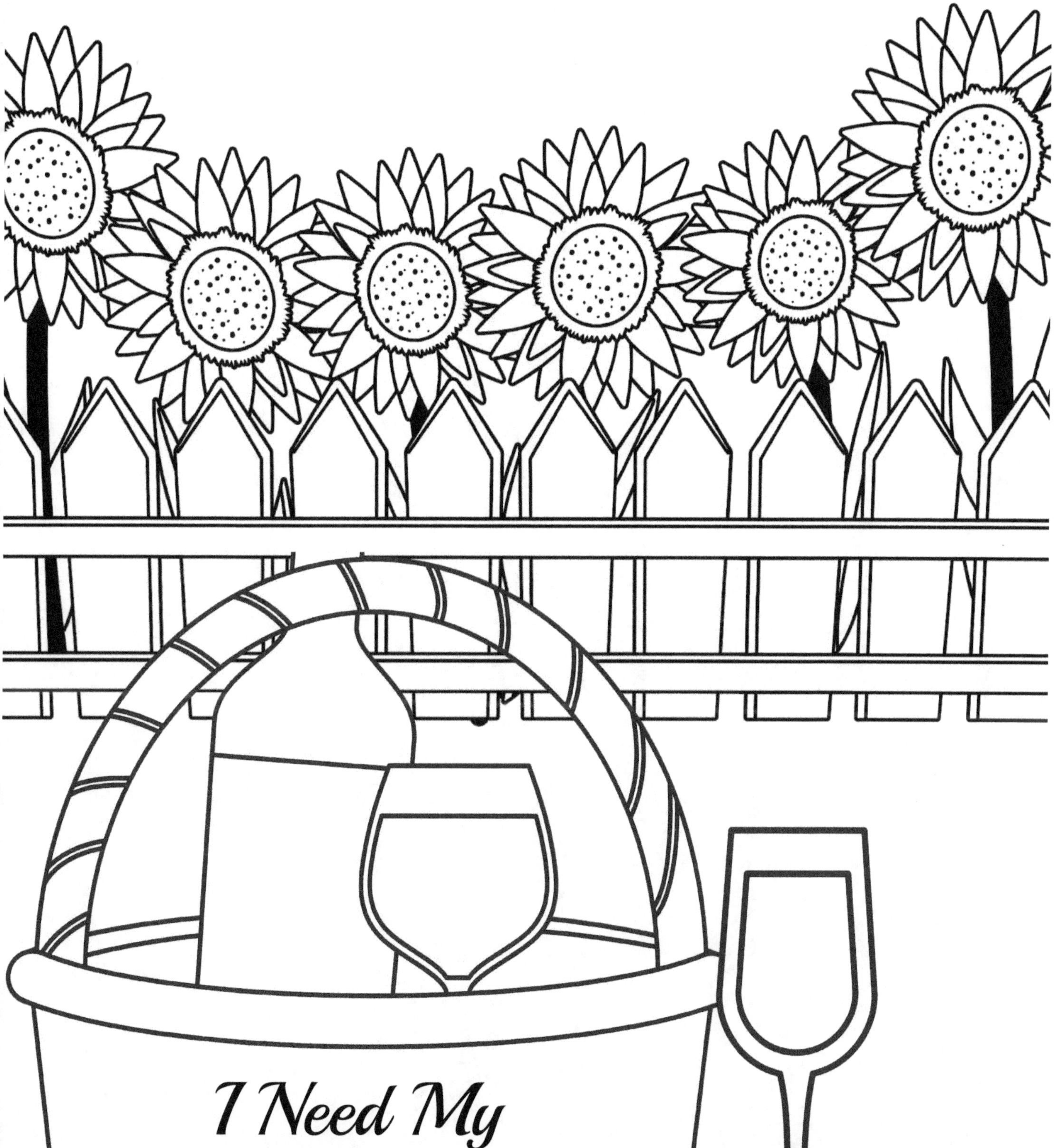
I Need My
Glasses

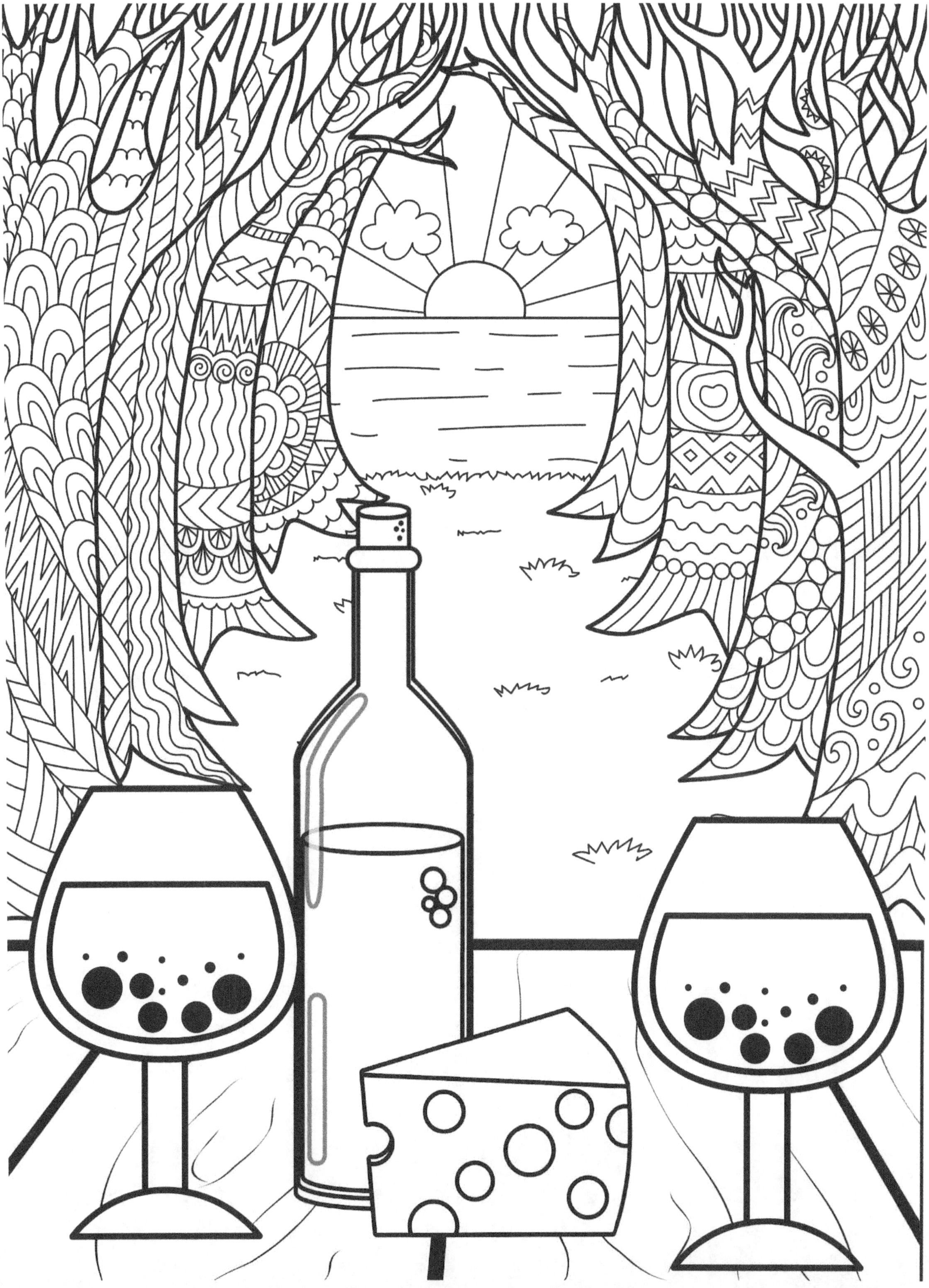

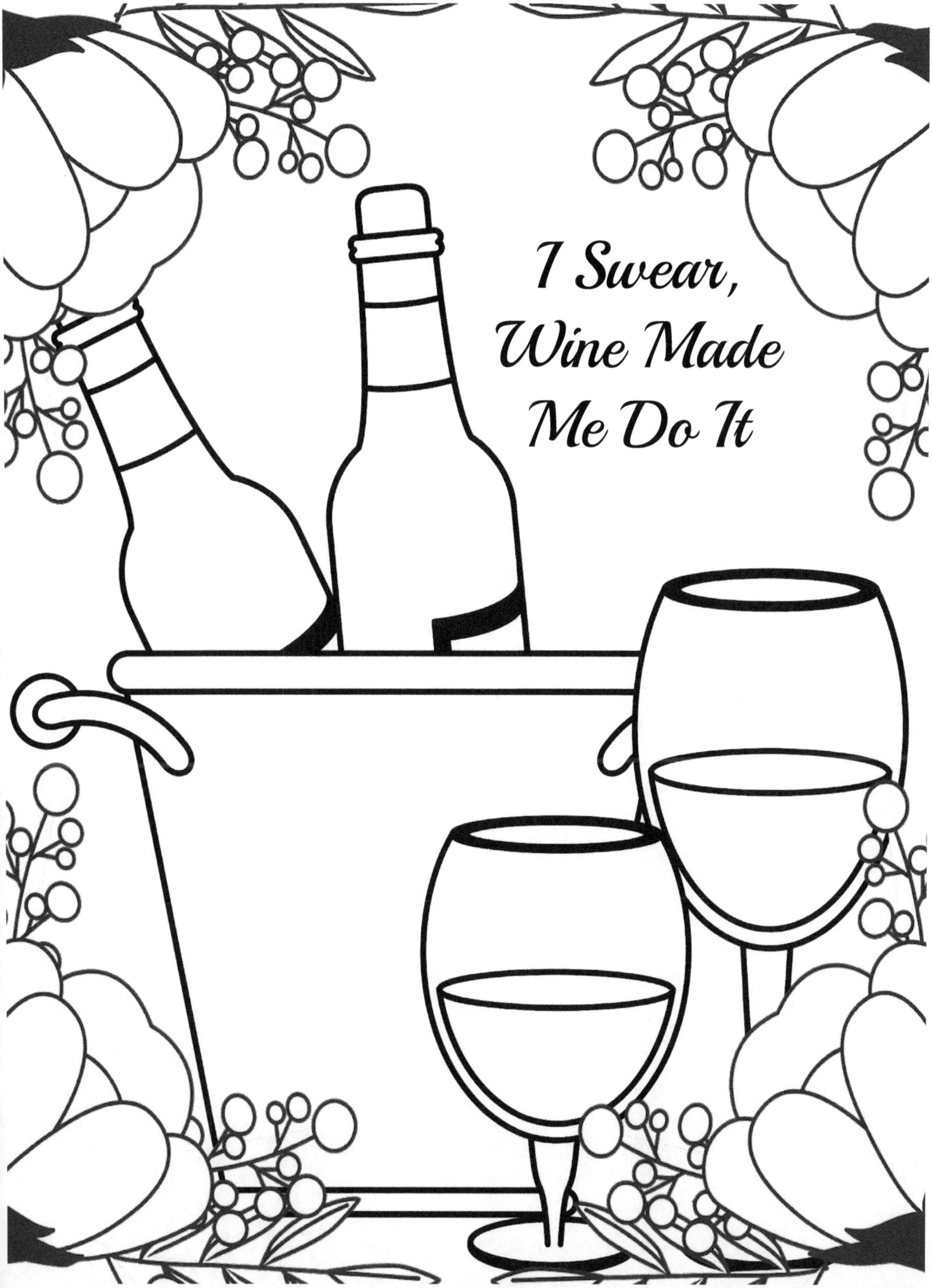
I Swear,
Wine Made
Me Do It

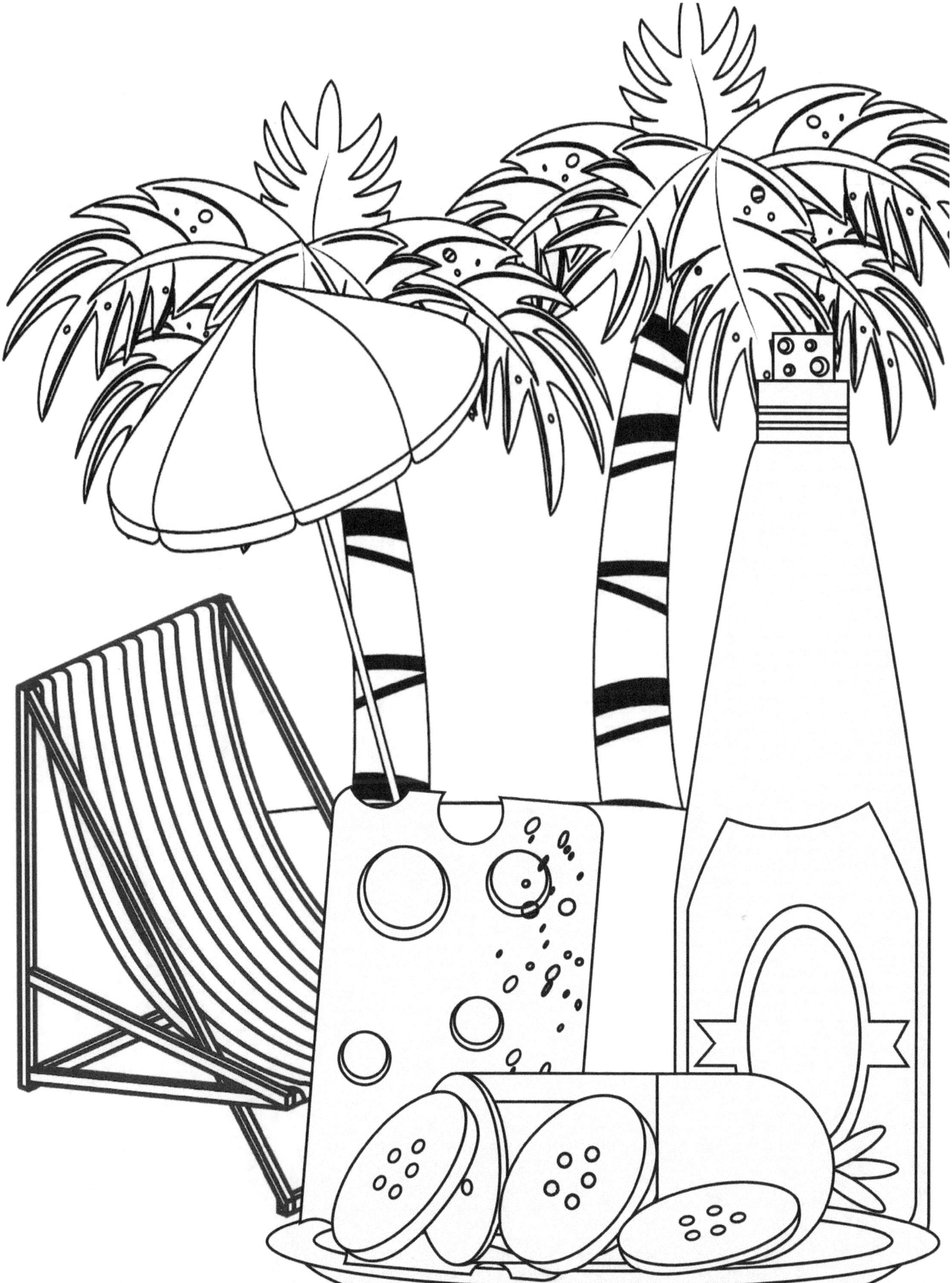

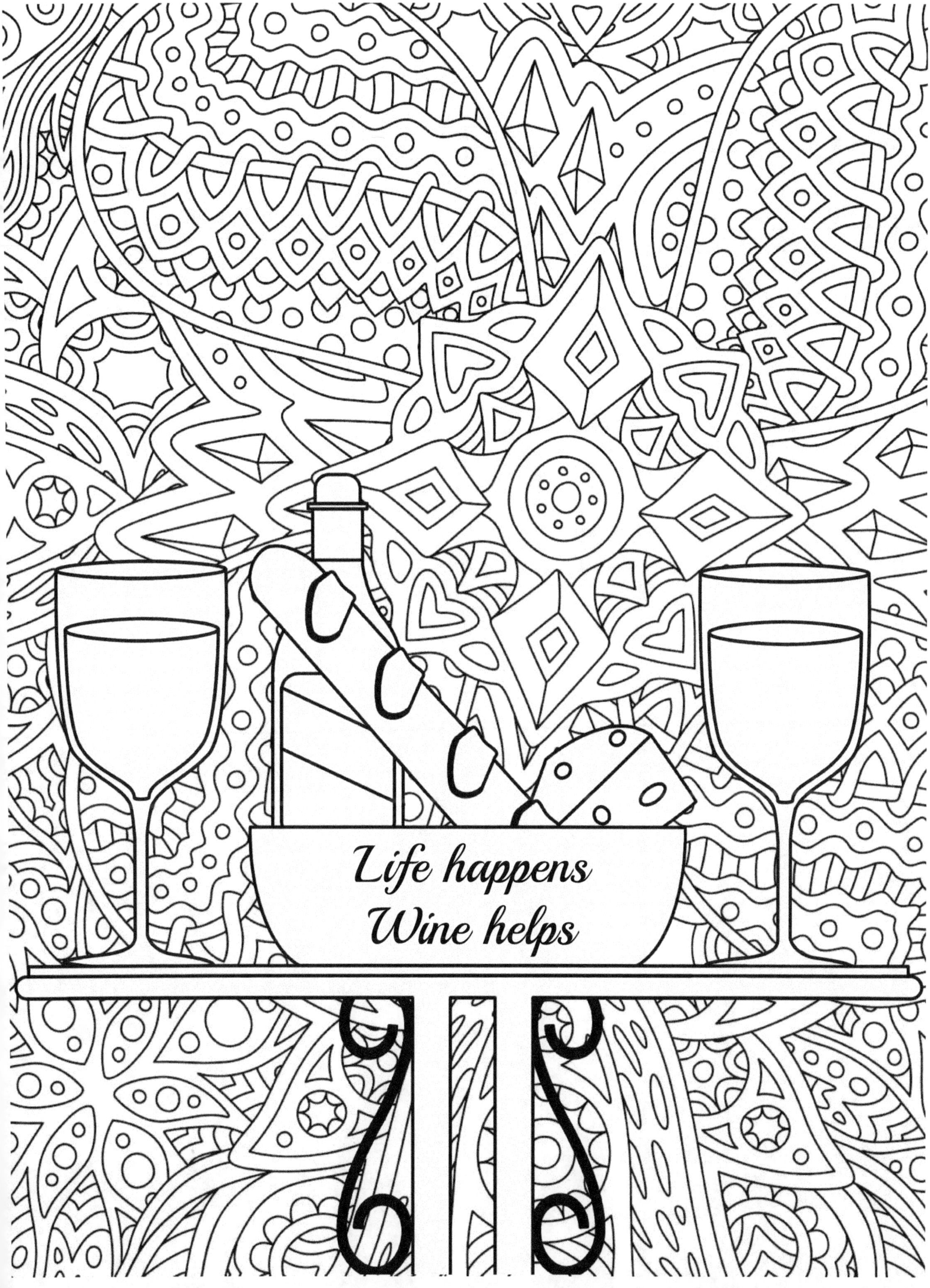
Life happens
Wine helps

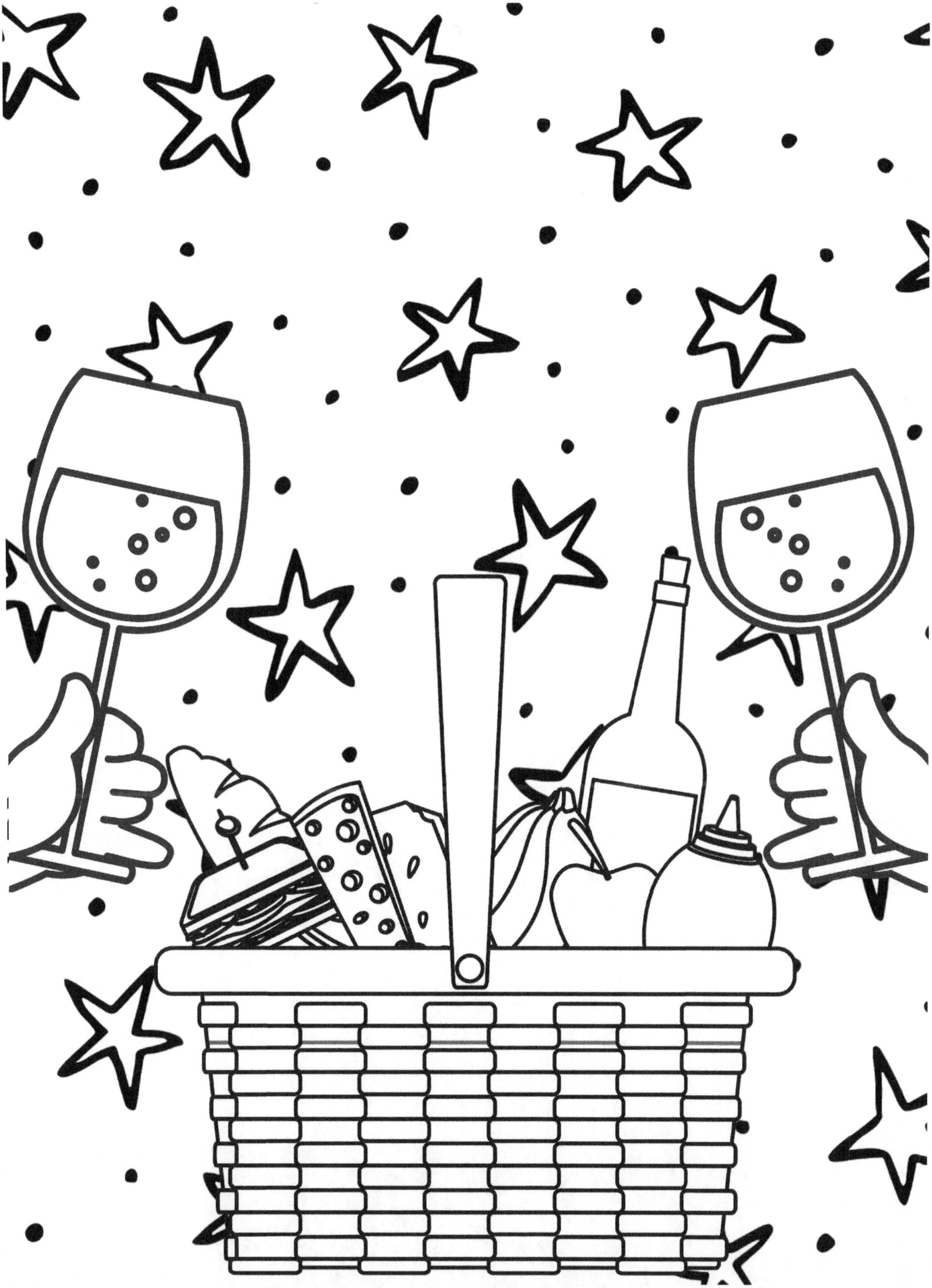

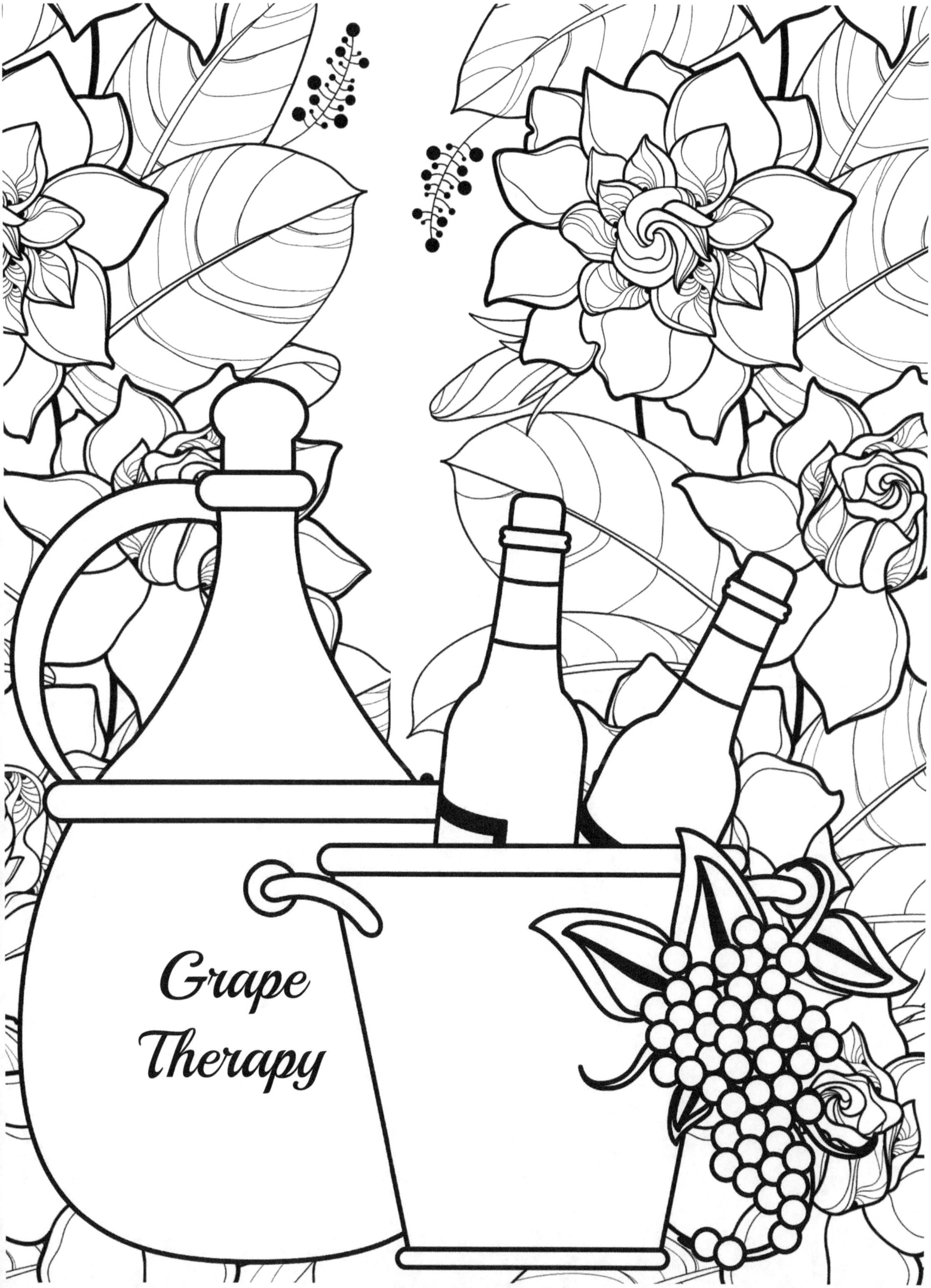
Grape
Therapy

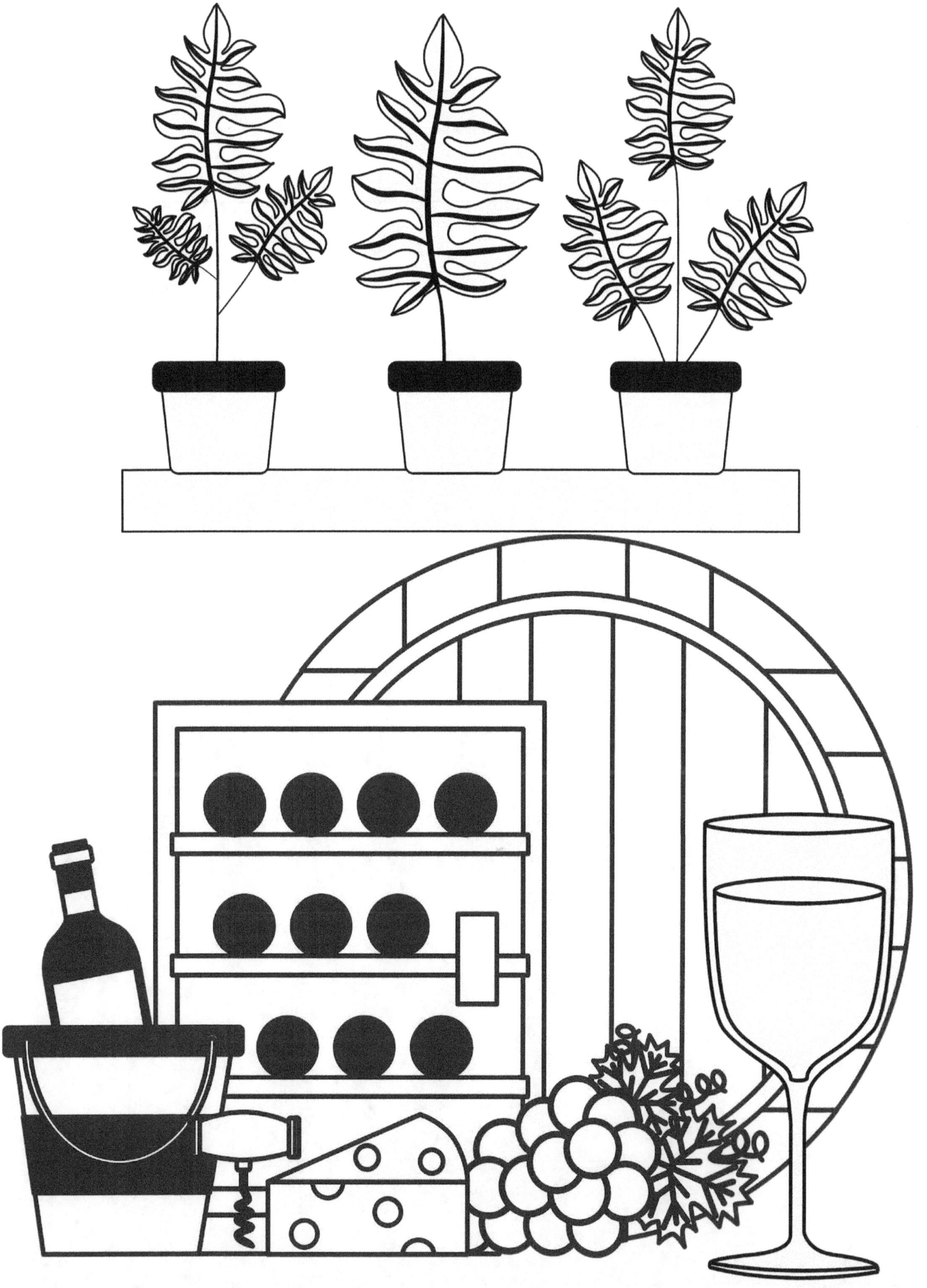

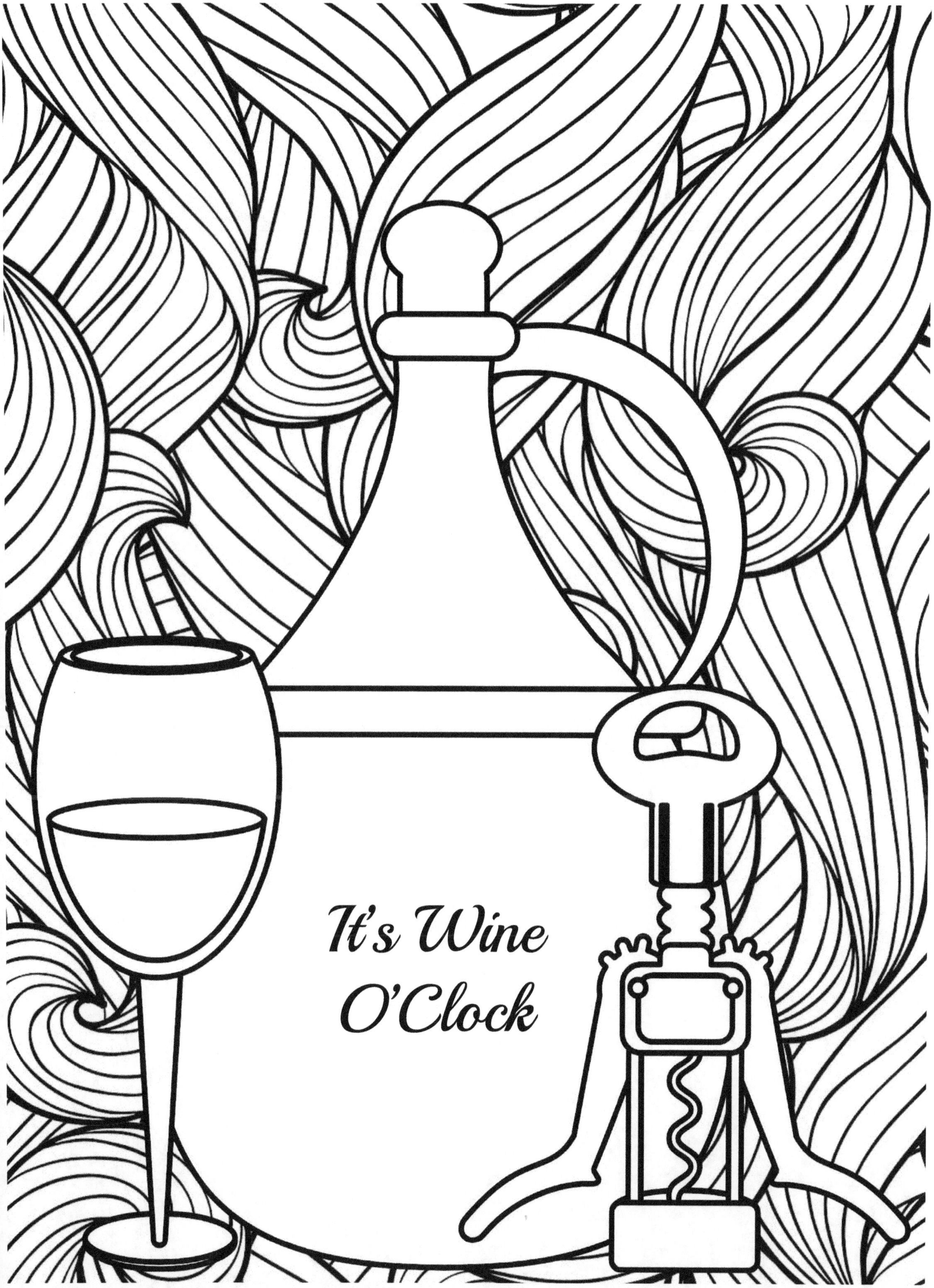
It's Wine
O'Clock

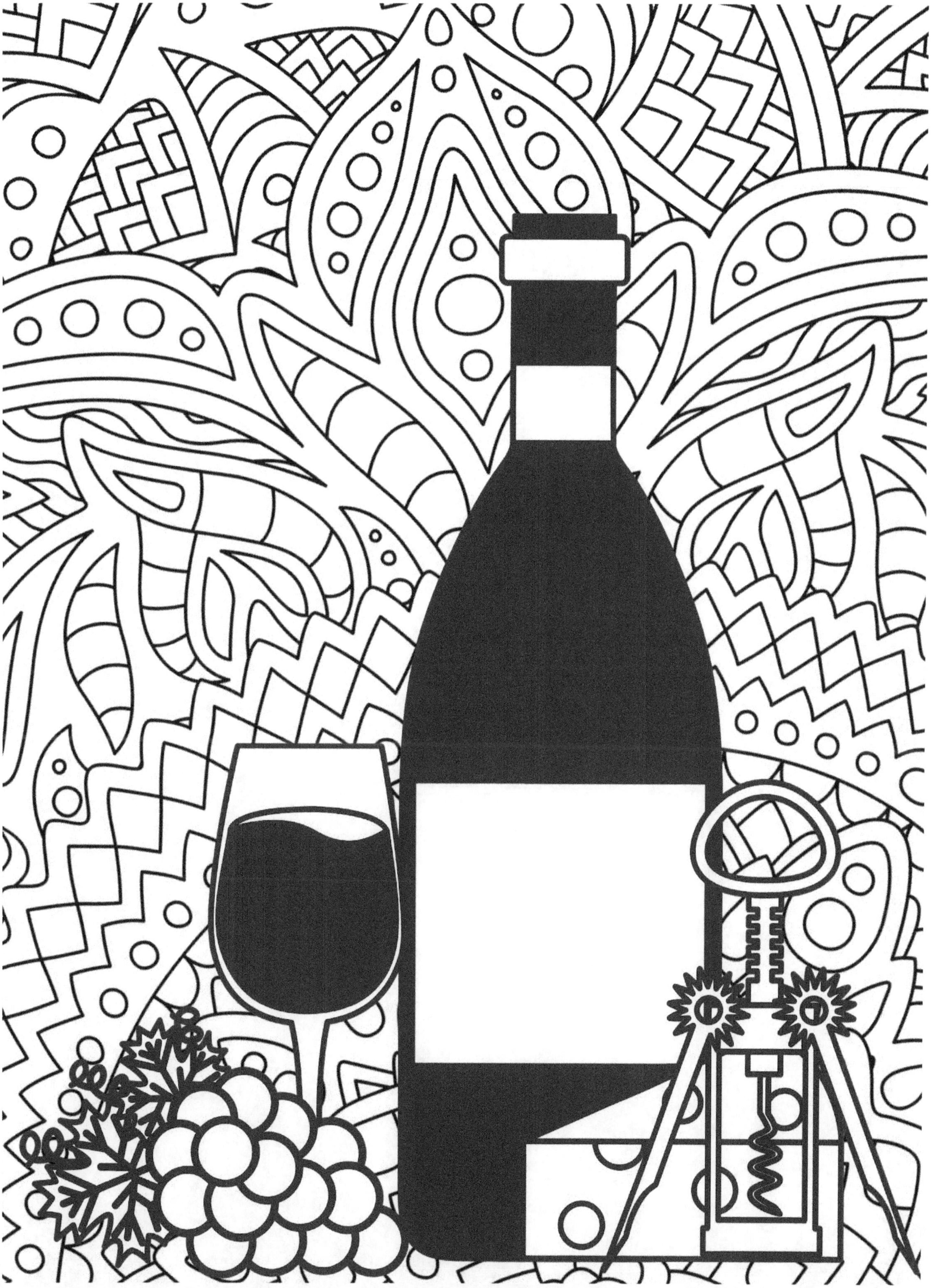

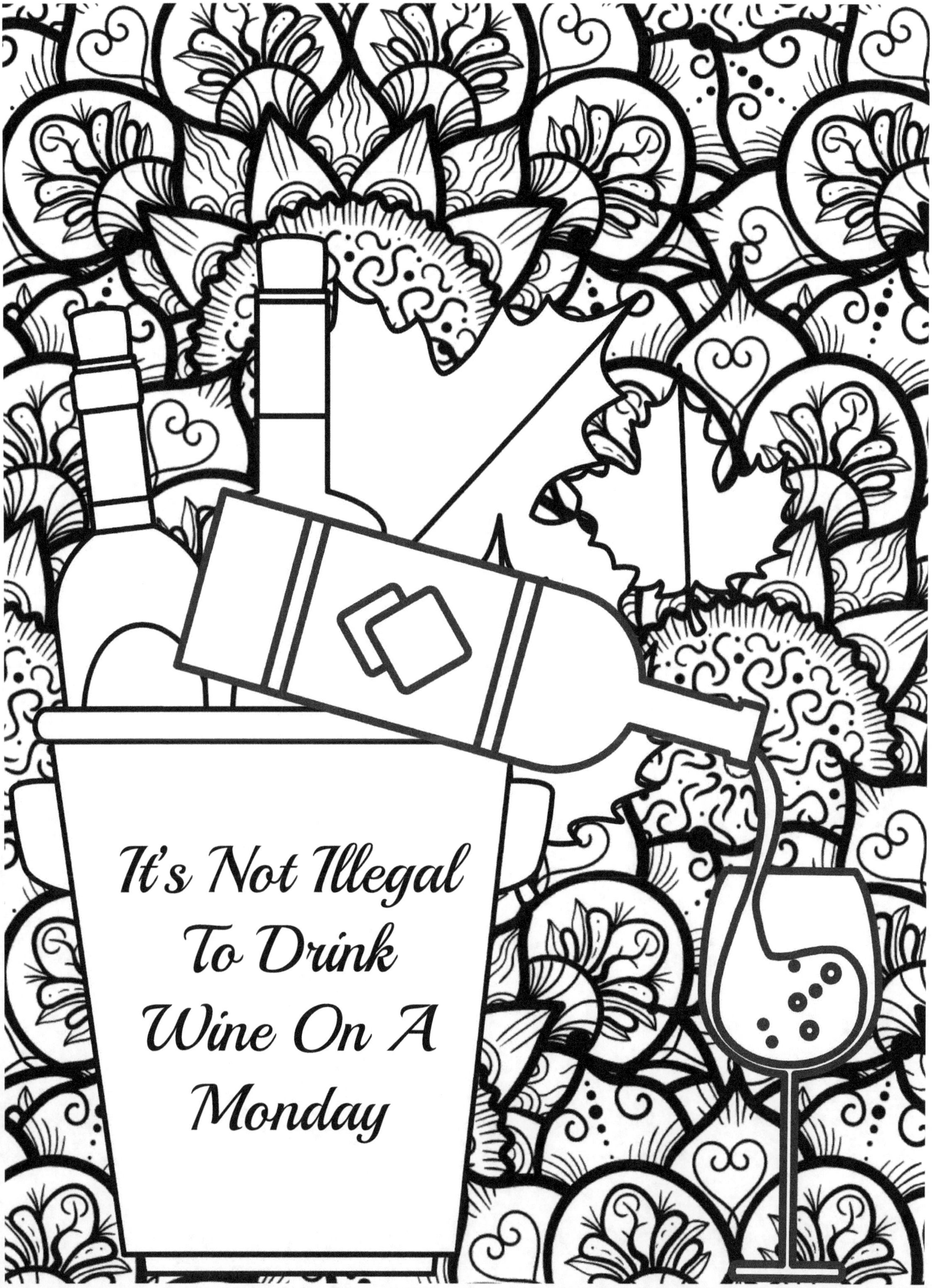
It's Not Illegal
To Drink
Wine On A
Monday

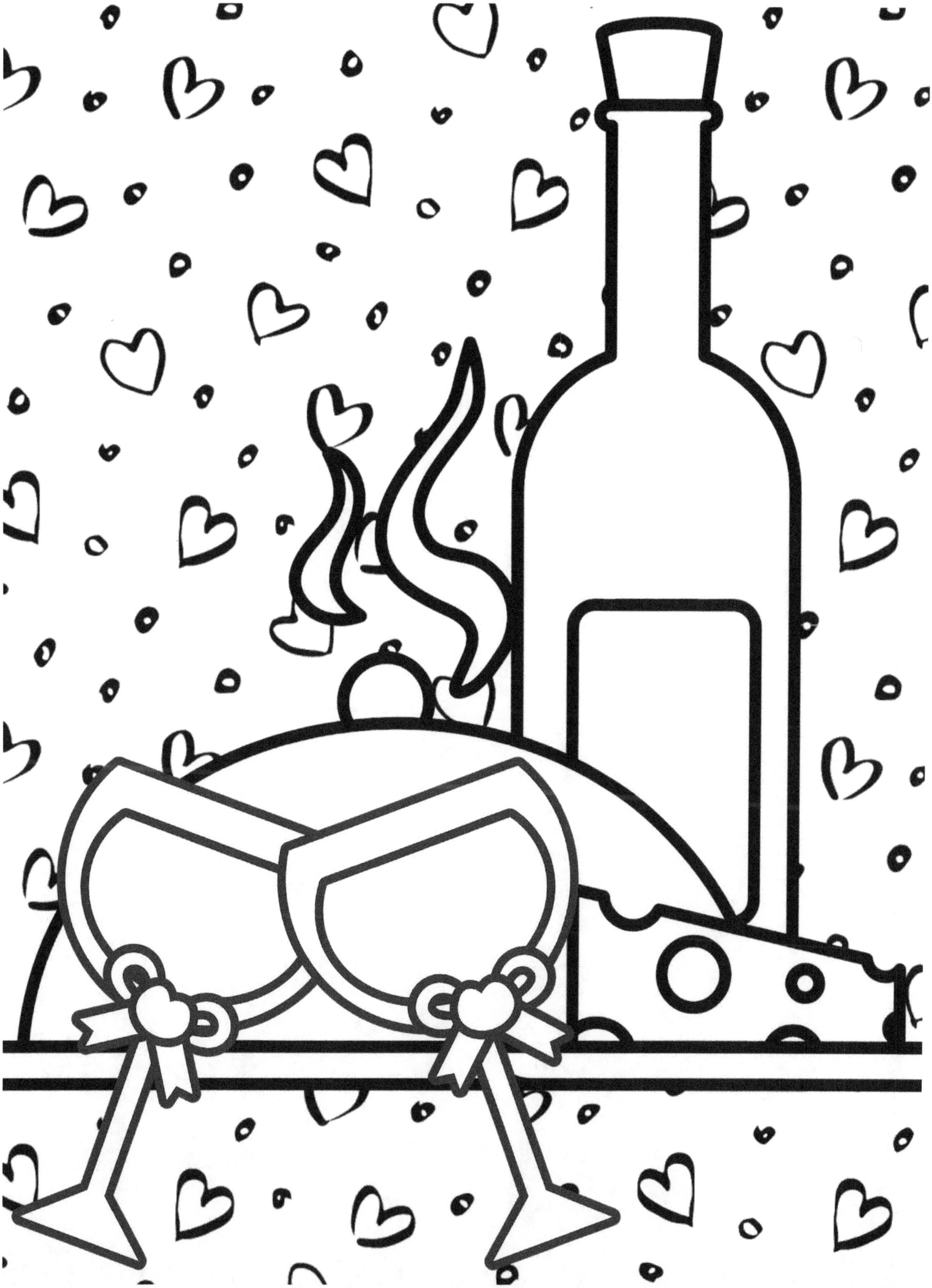

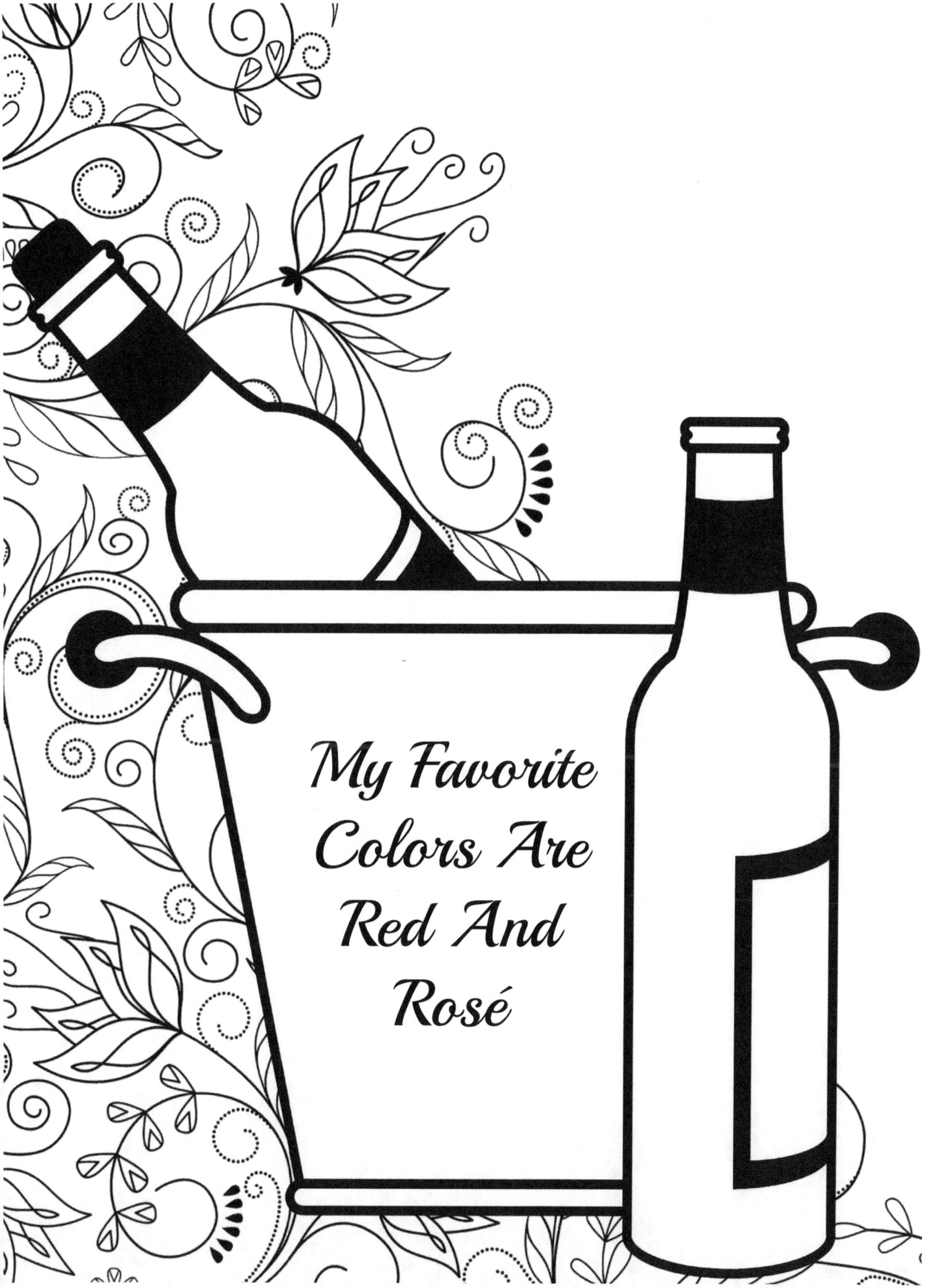
My Favorite
Colors Are
Red And
Rosé

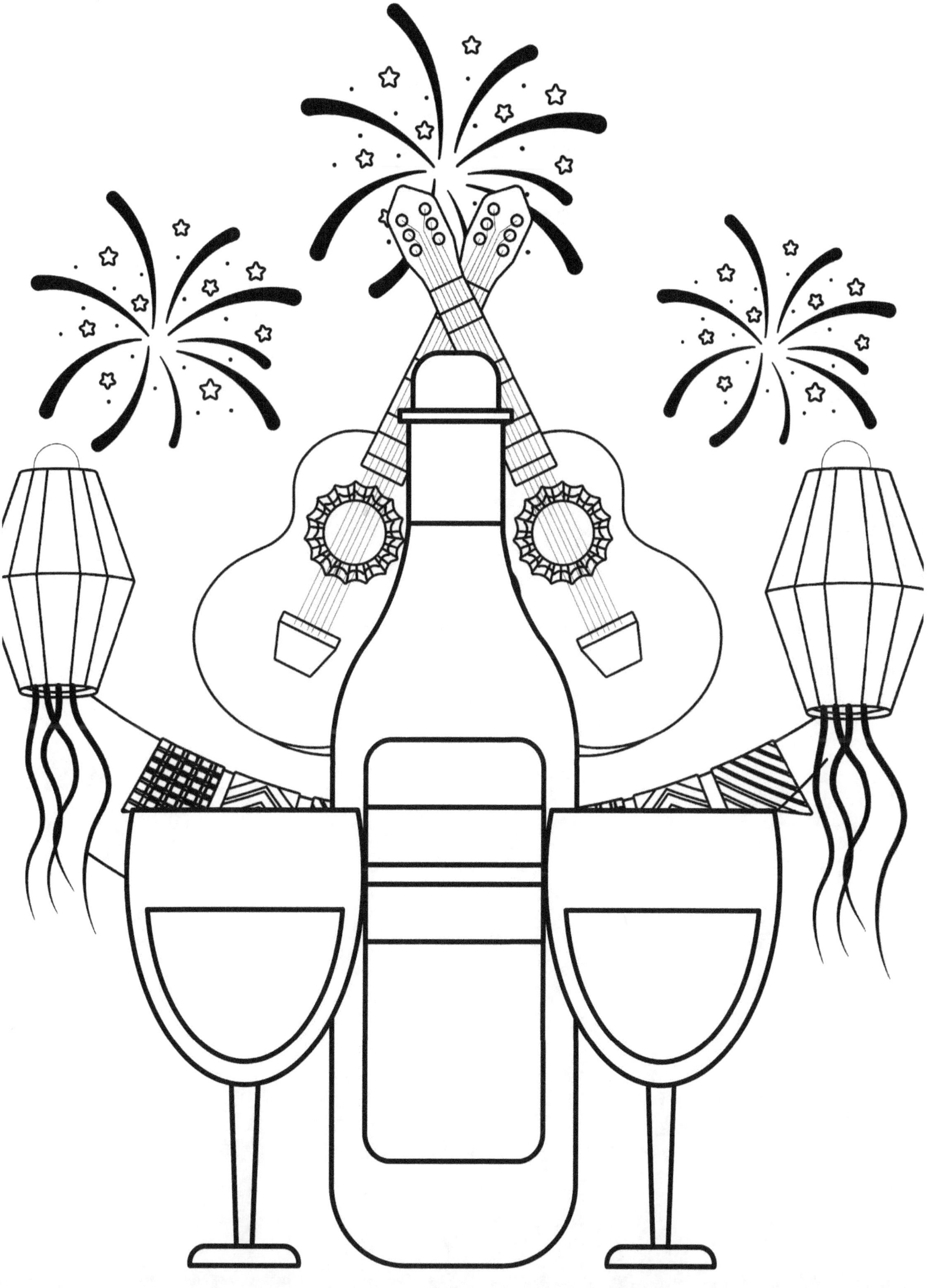

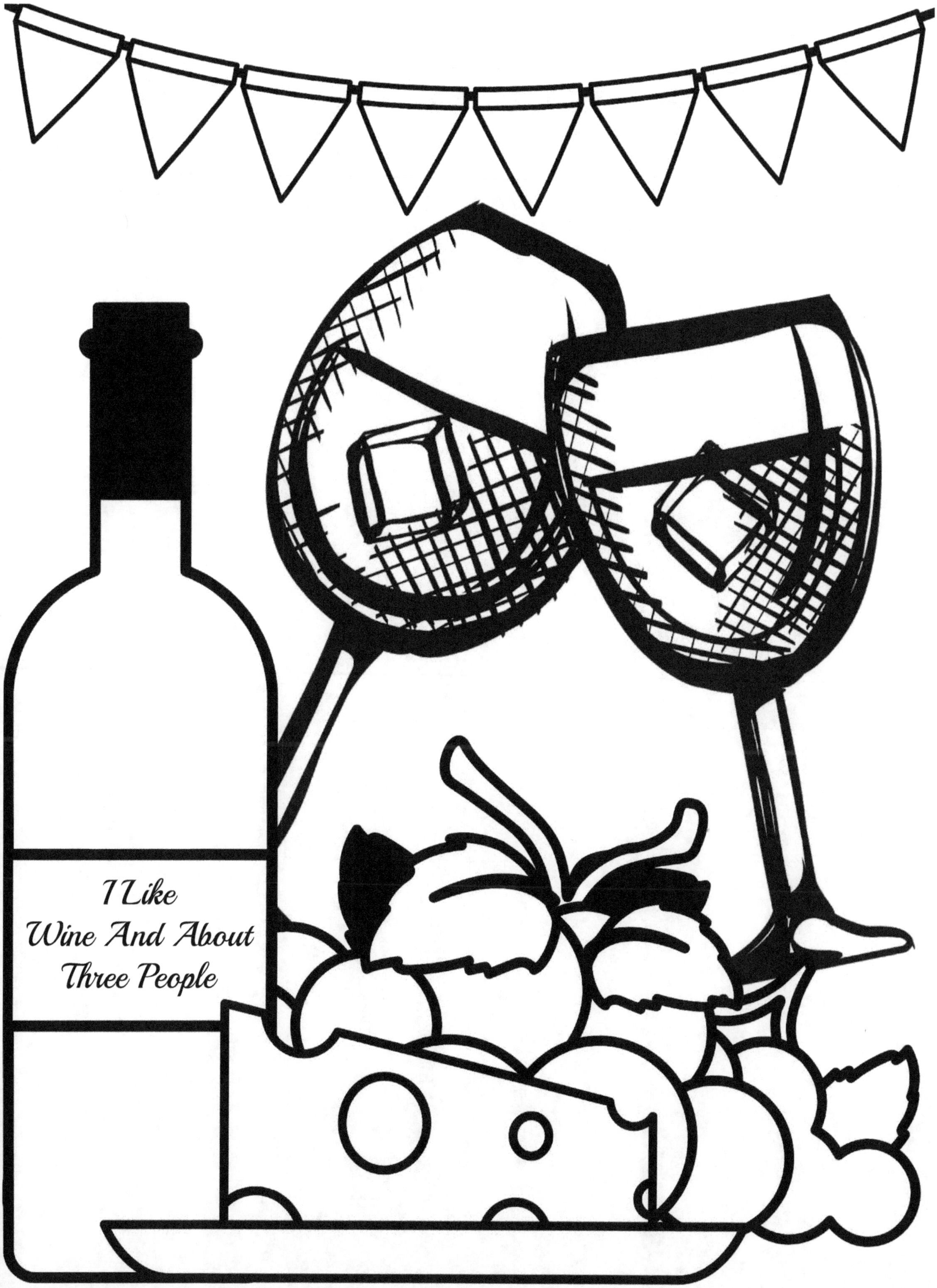
I Like
Wine And About
Three People

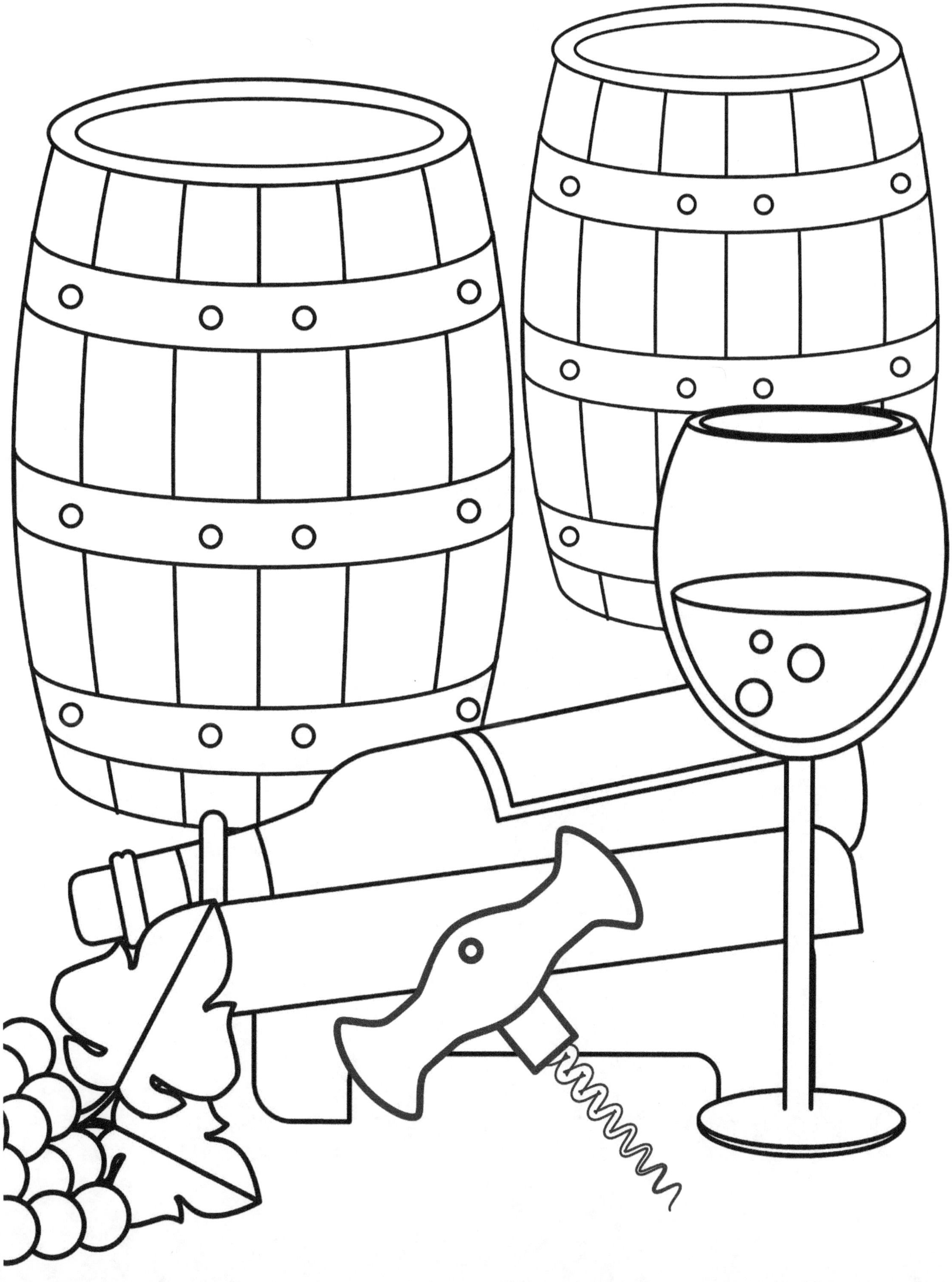

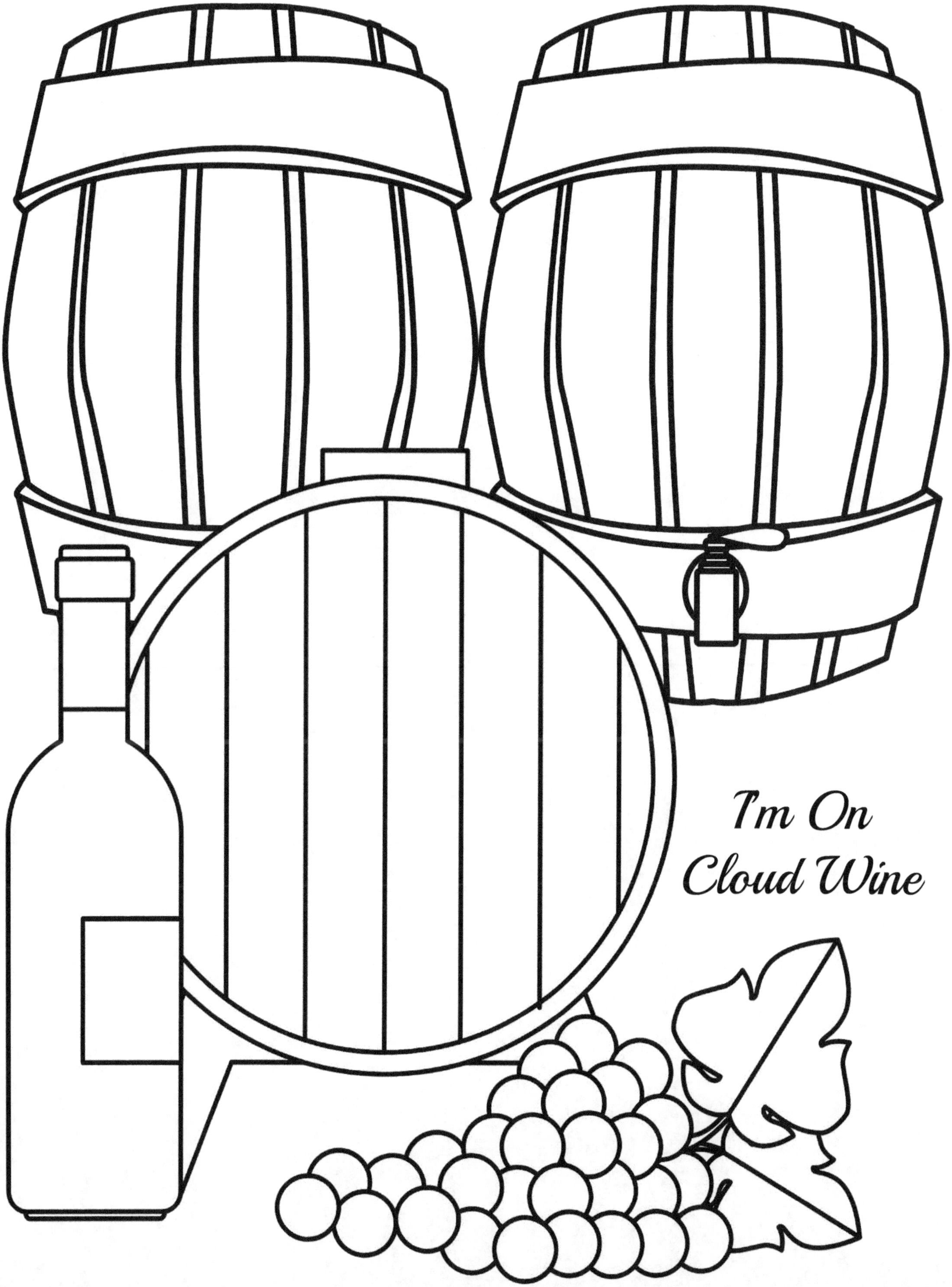
I'm On
Cloud Wine

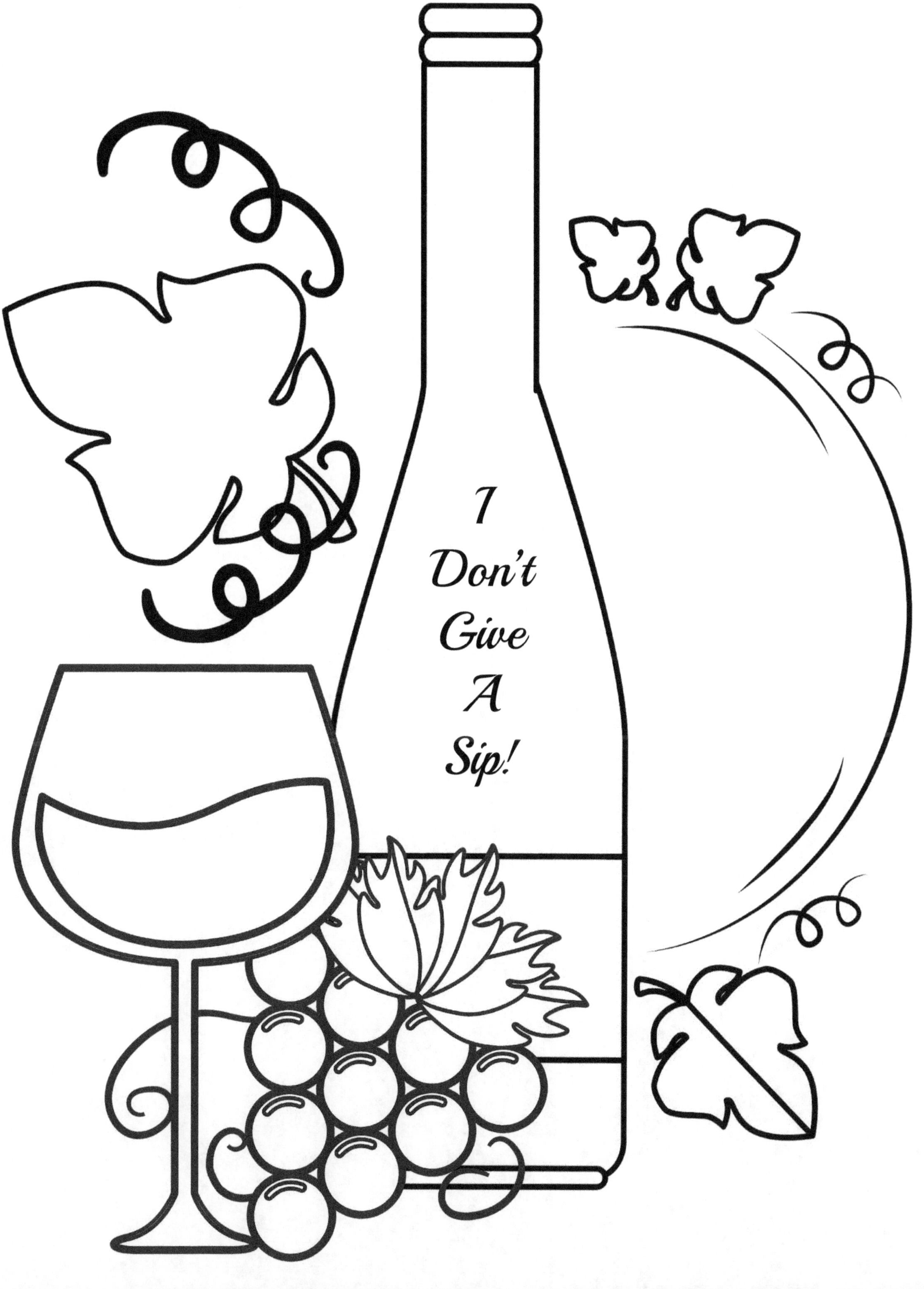
I
Don't
Give
A
Sip!

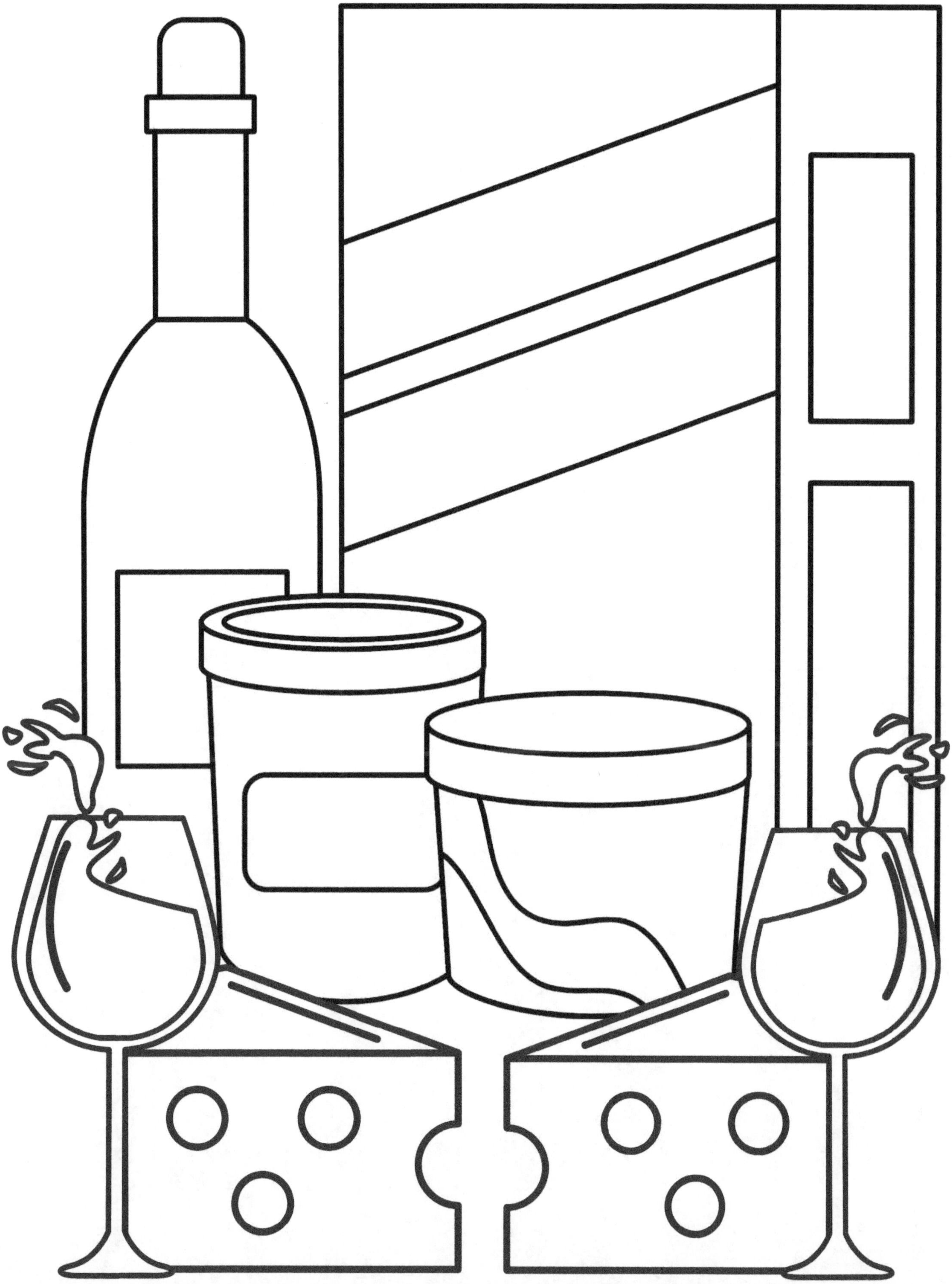

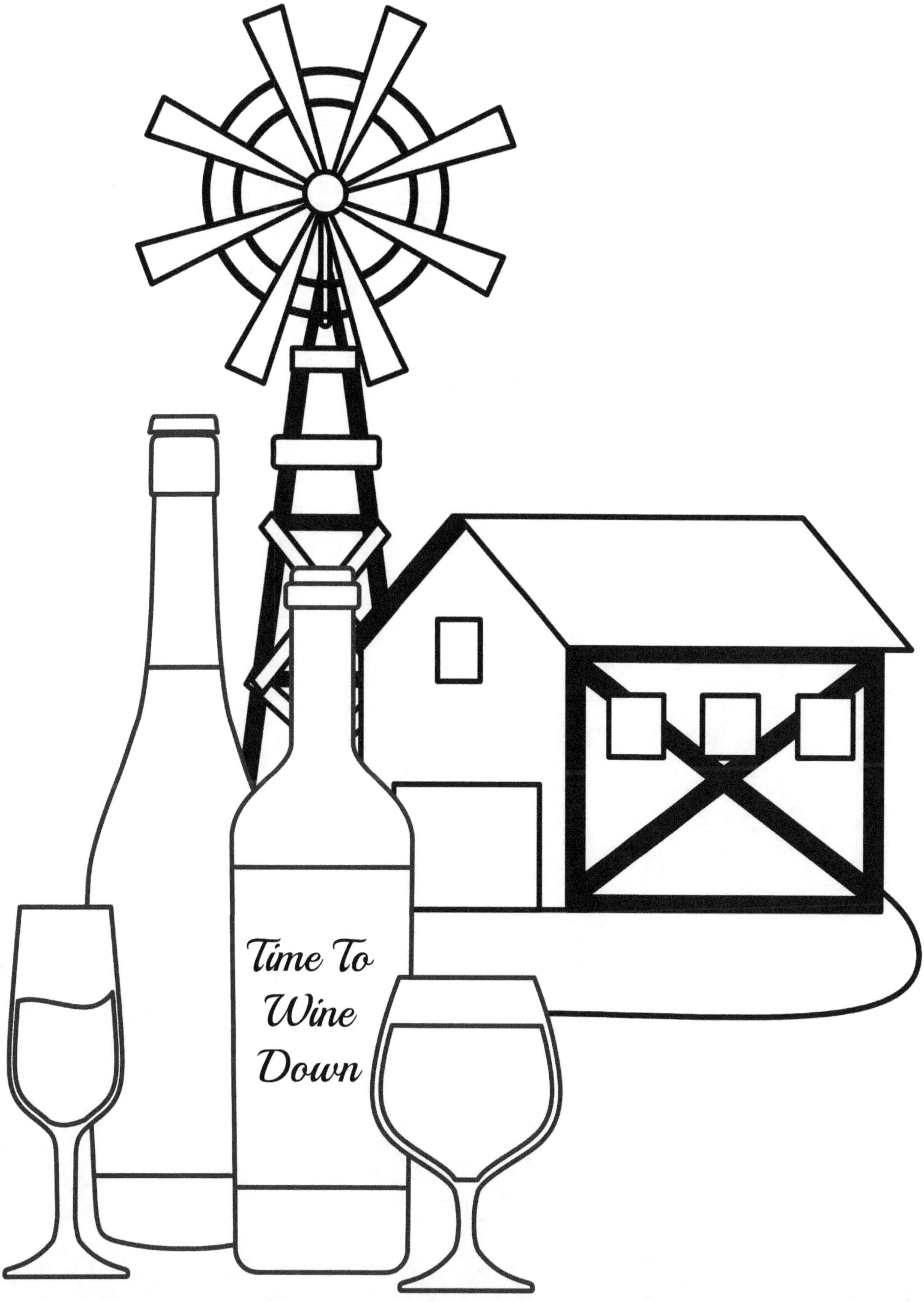
Time To
Wine
Down

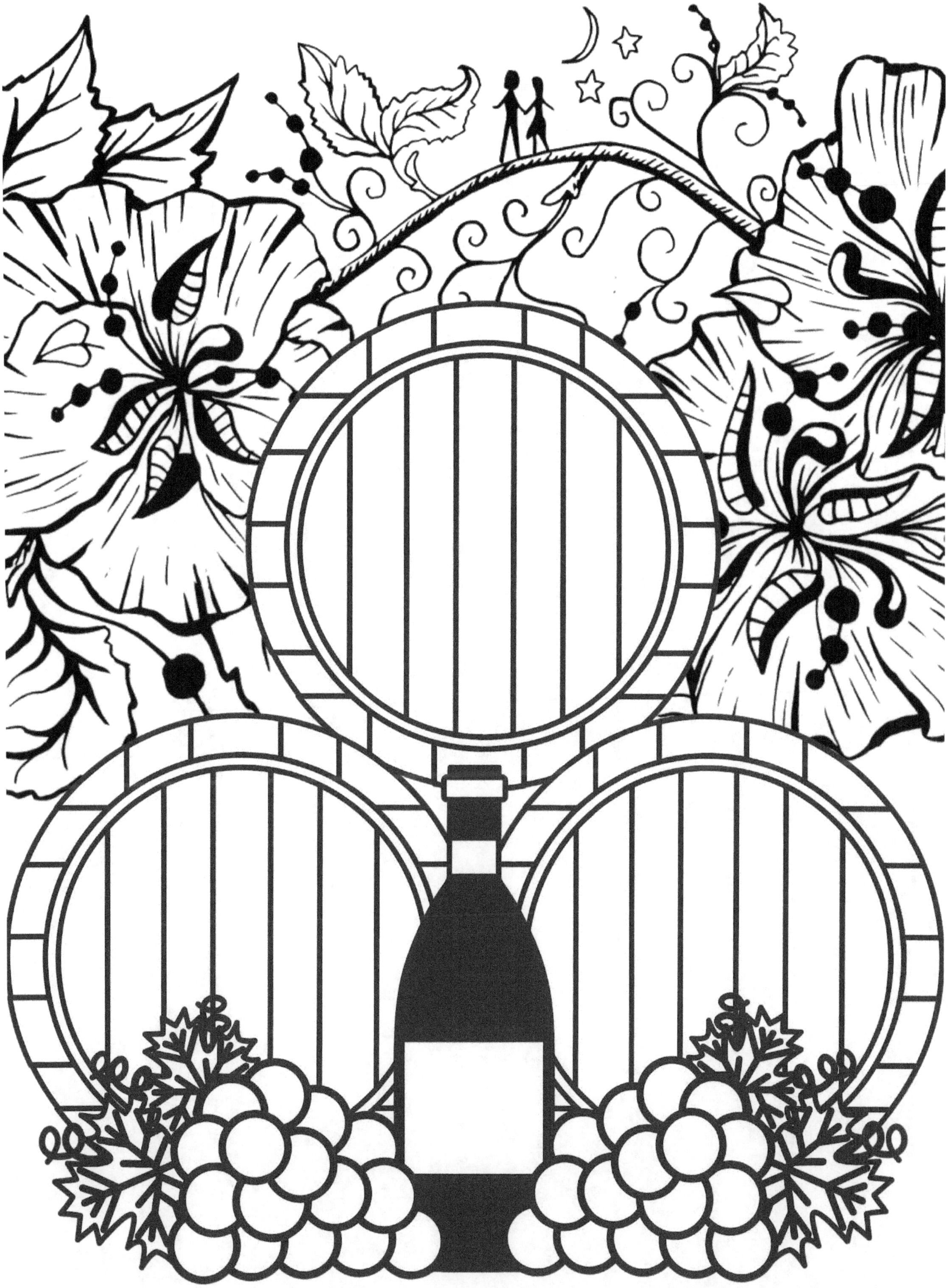

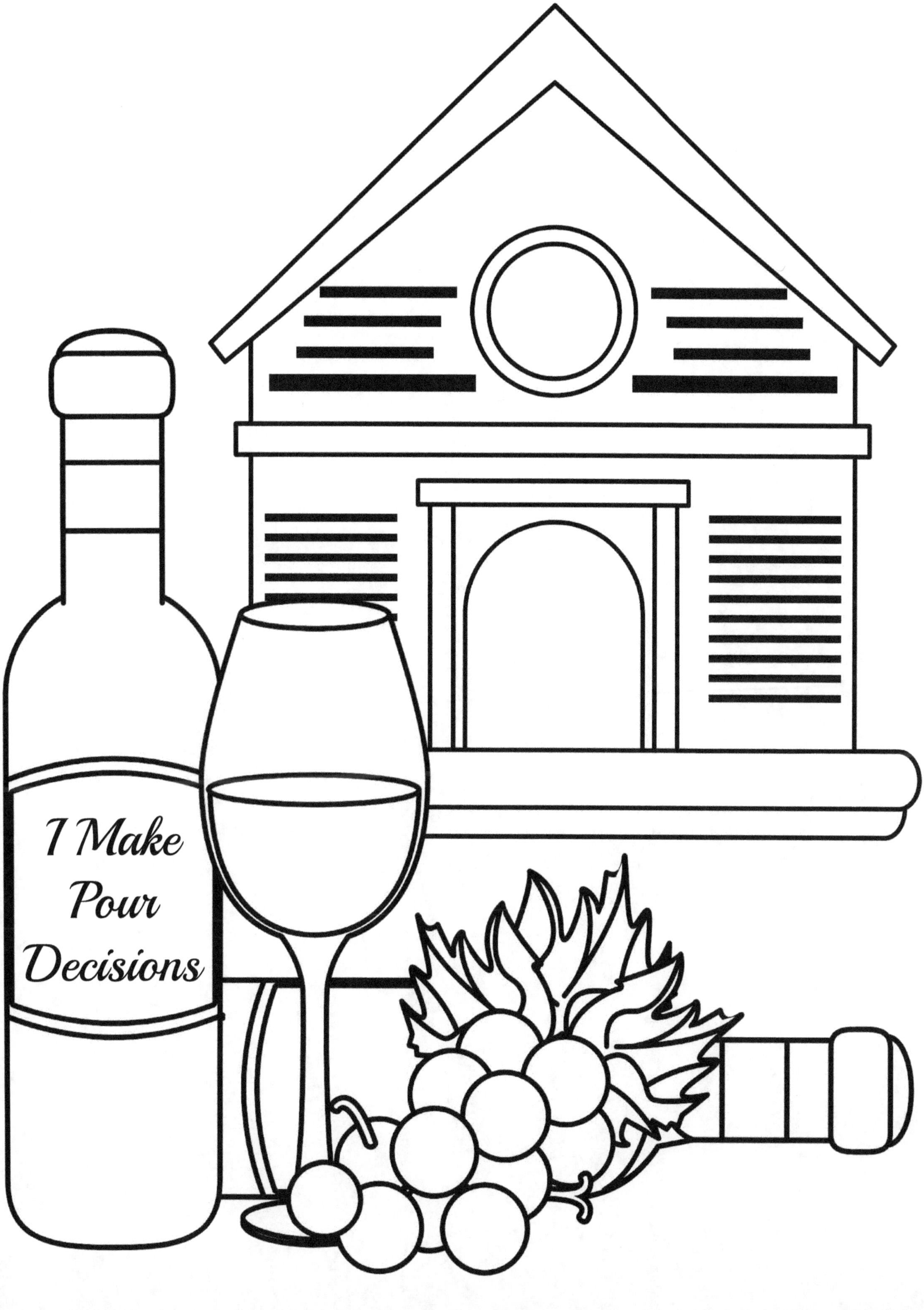
I Make
Pour
Decisions

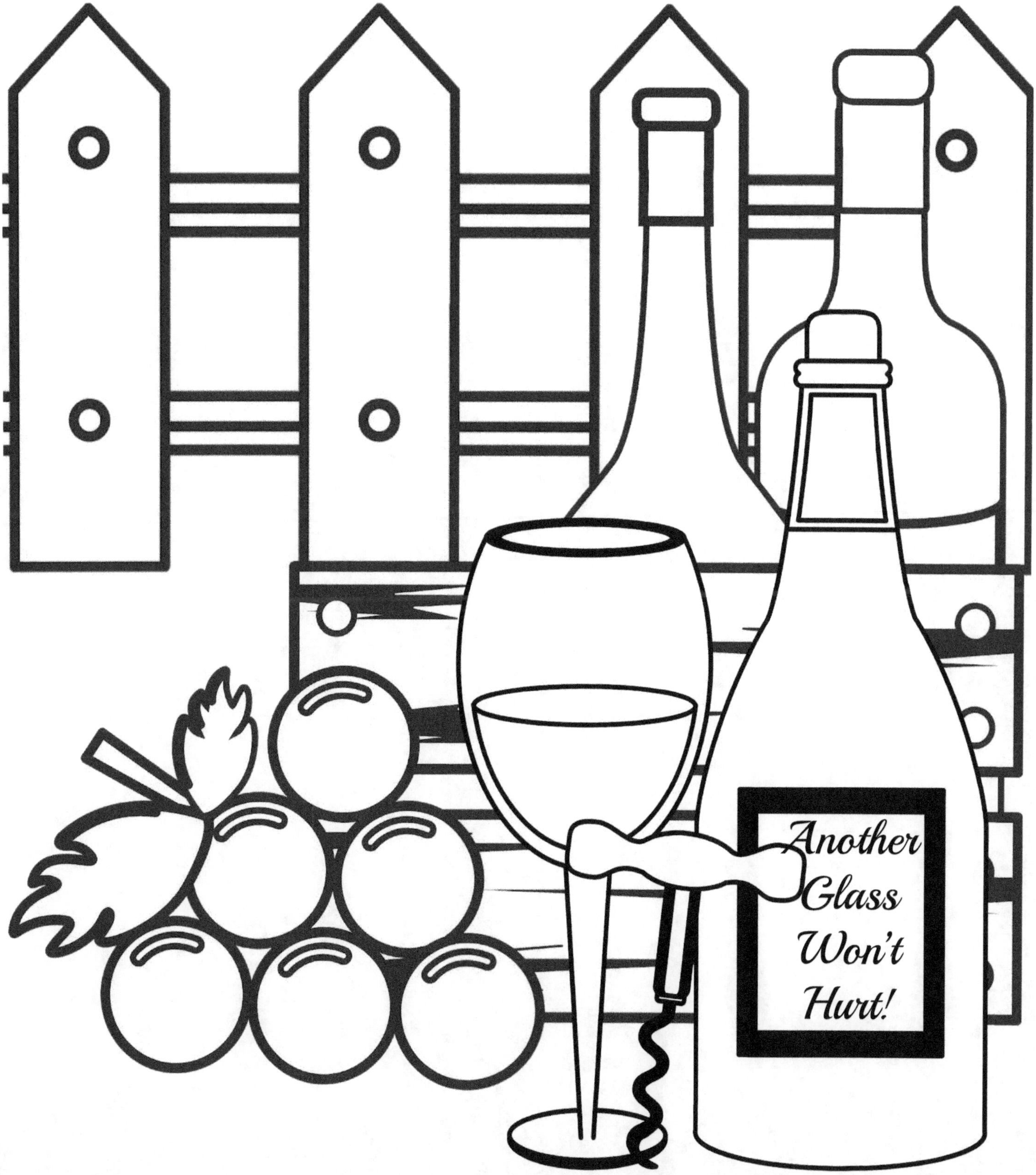
Another
Glass
Won't
Hurt!

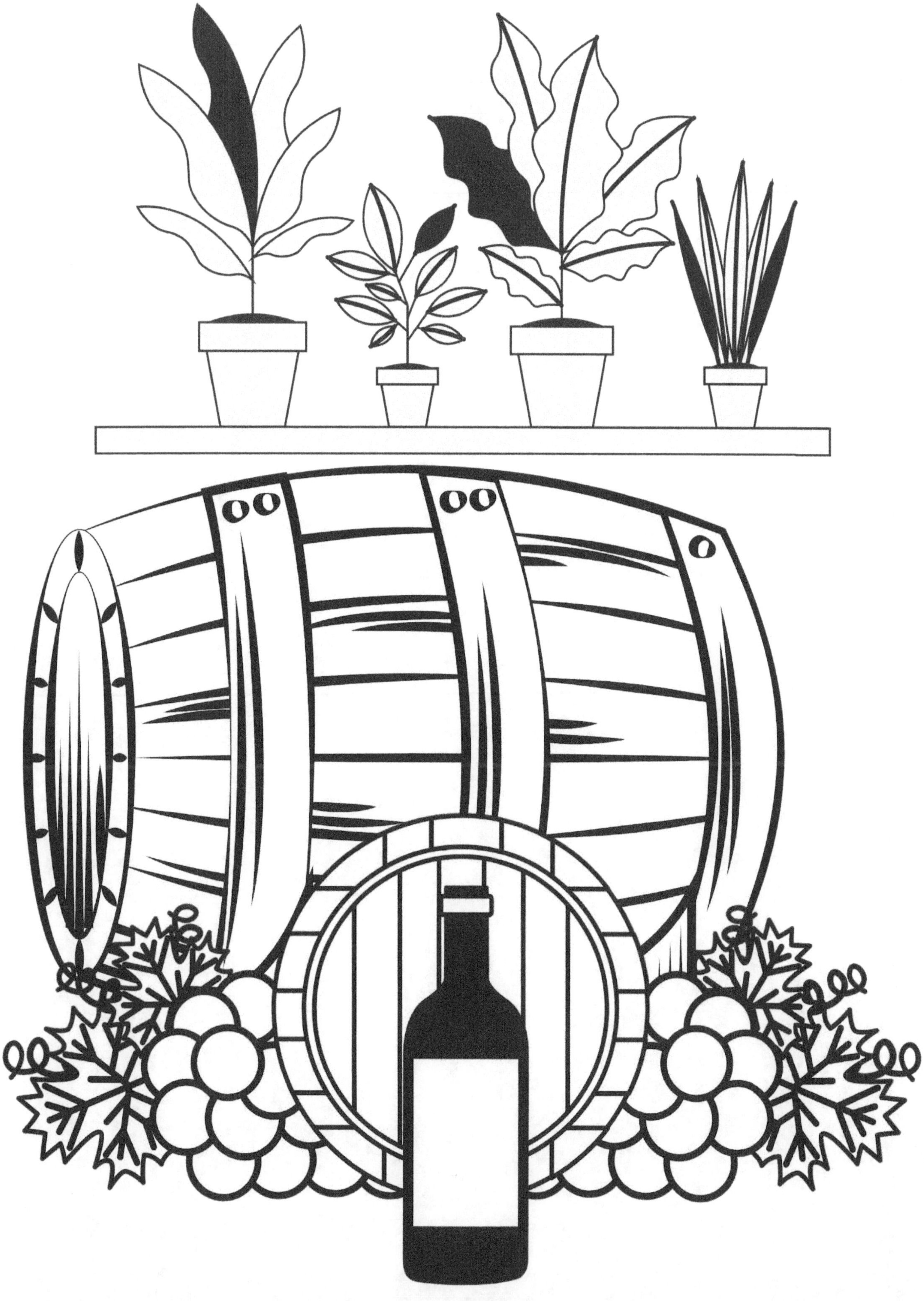

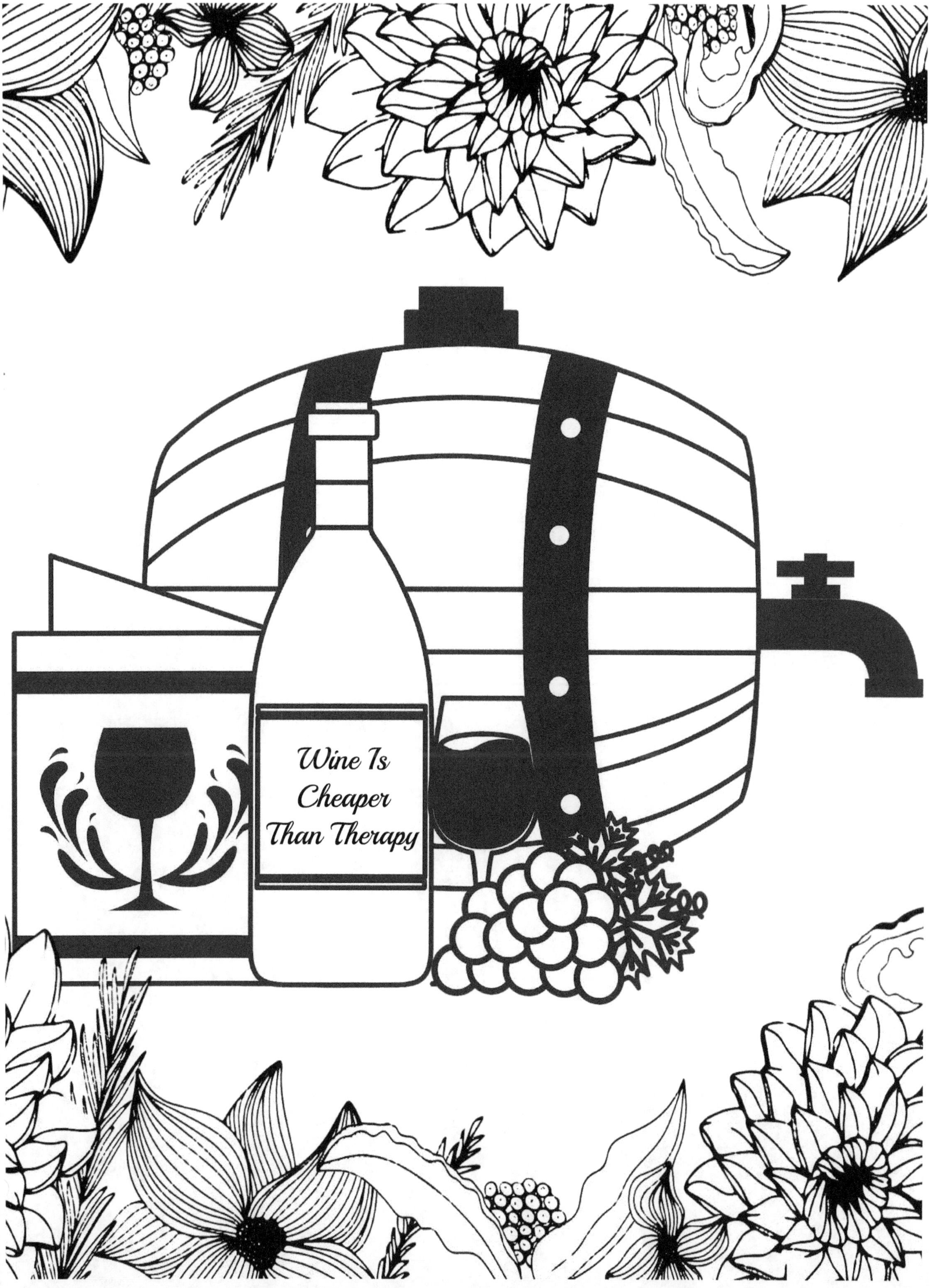
Wine Is
Cheaper
Than Therapy

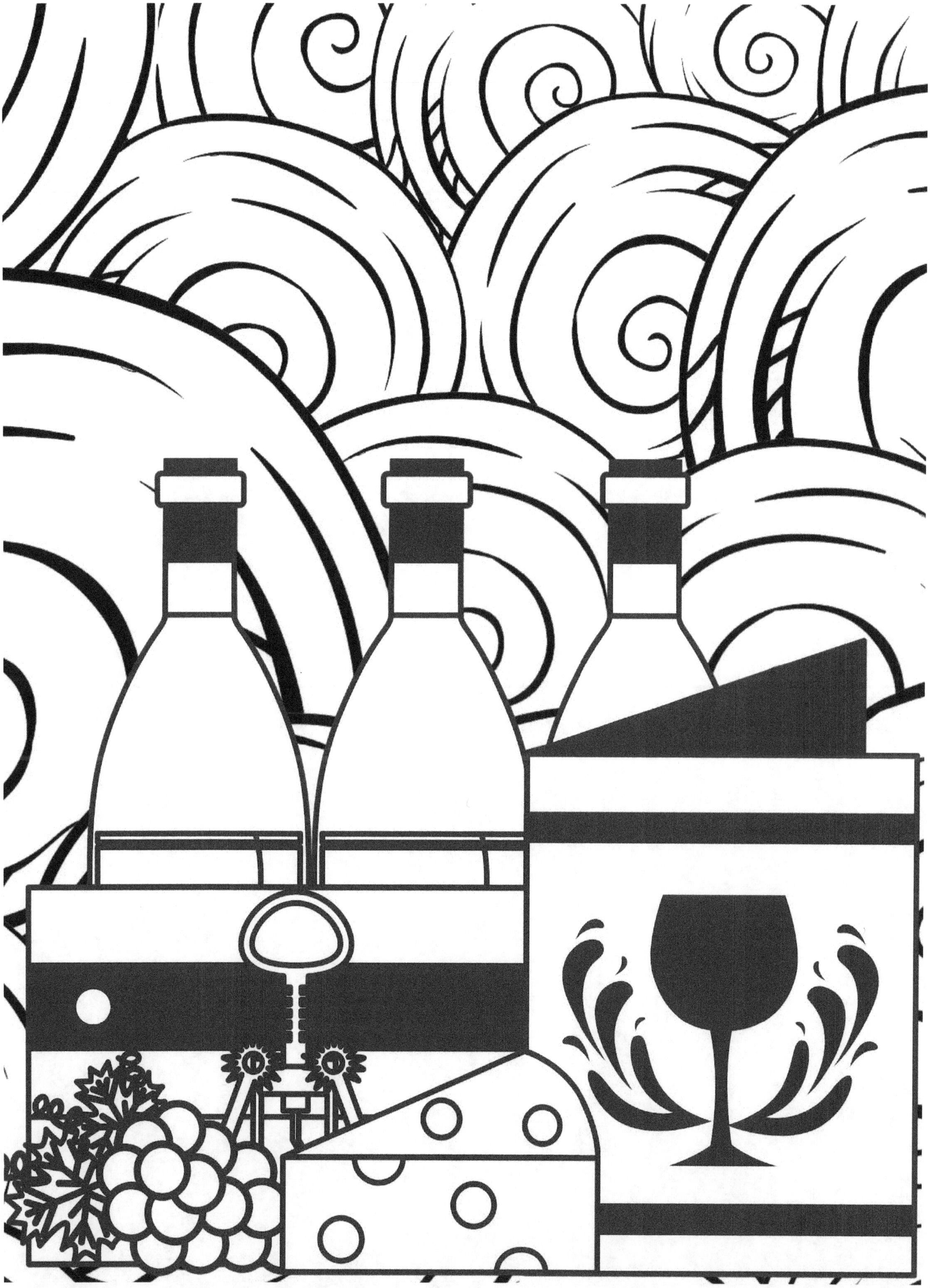

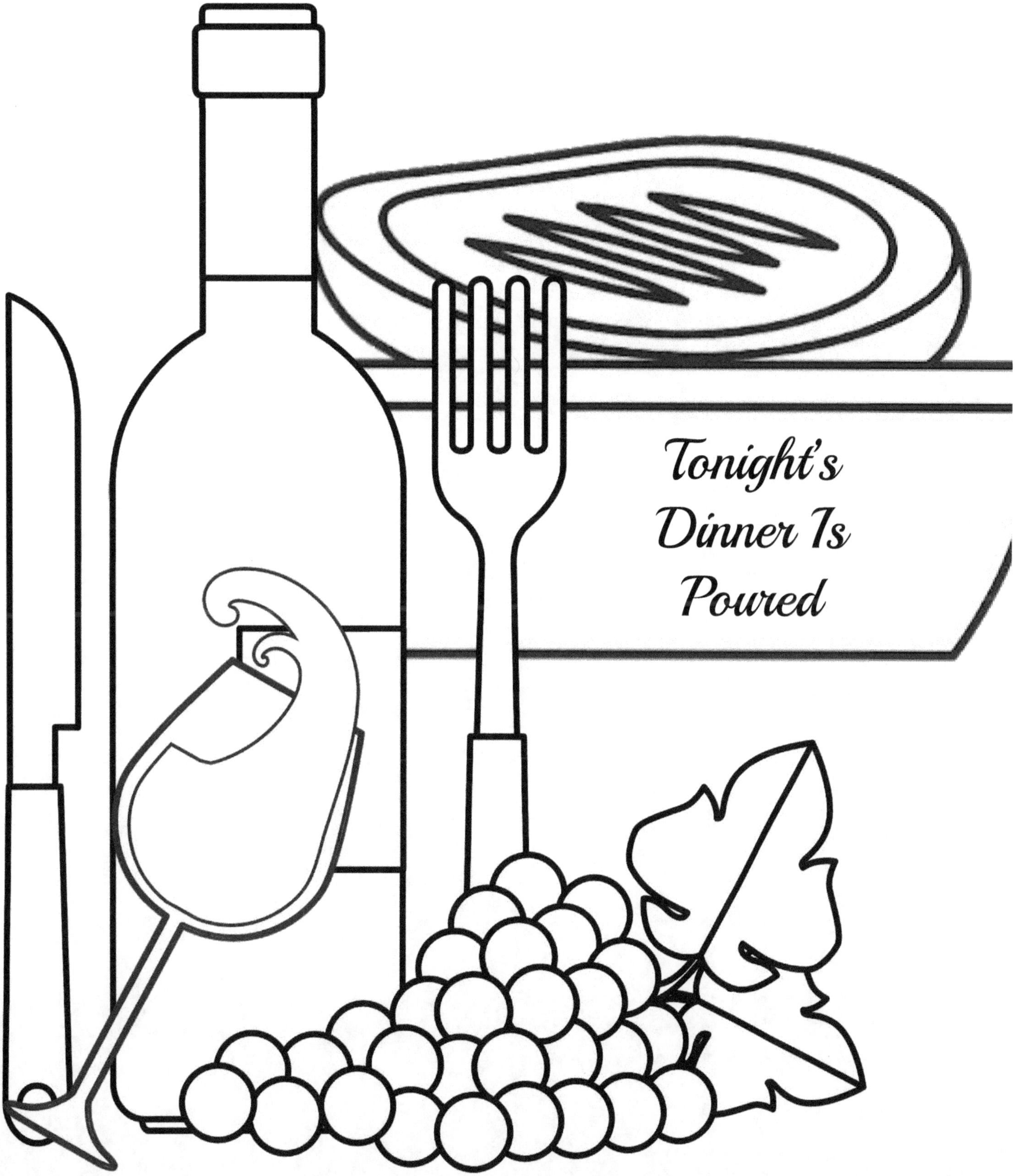
Tonight's
Dinner Is
Poured

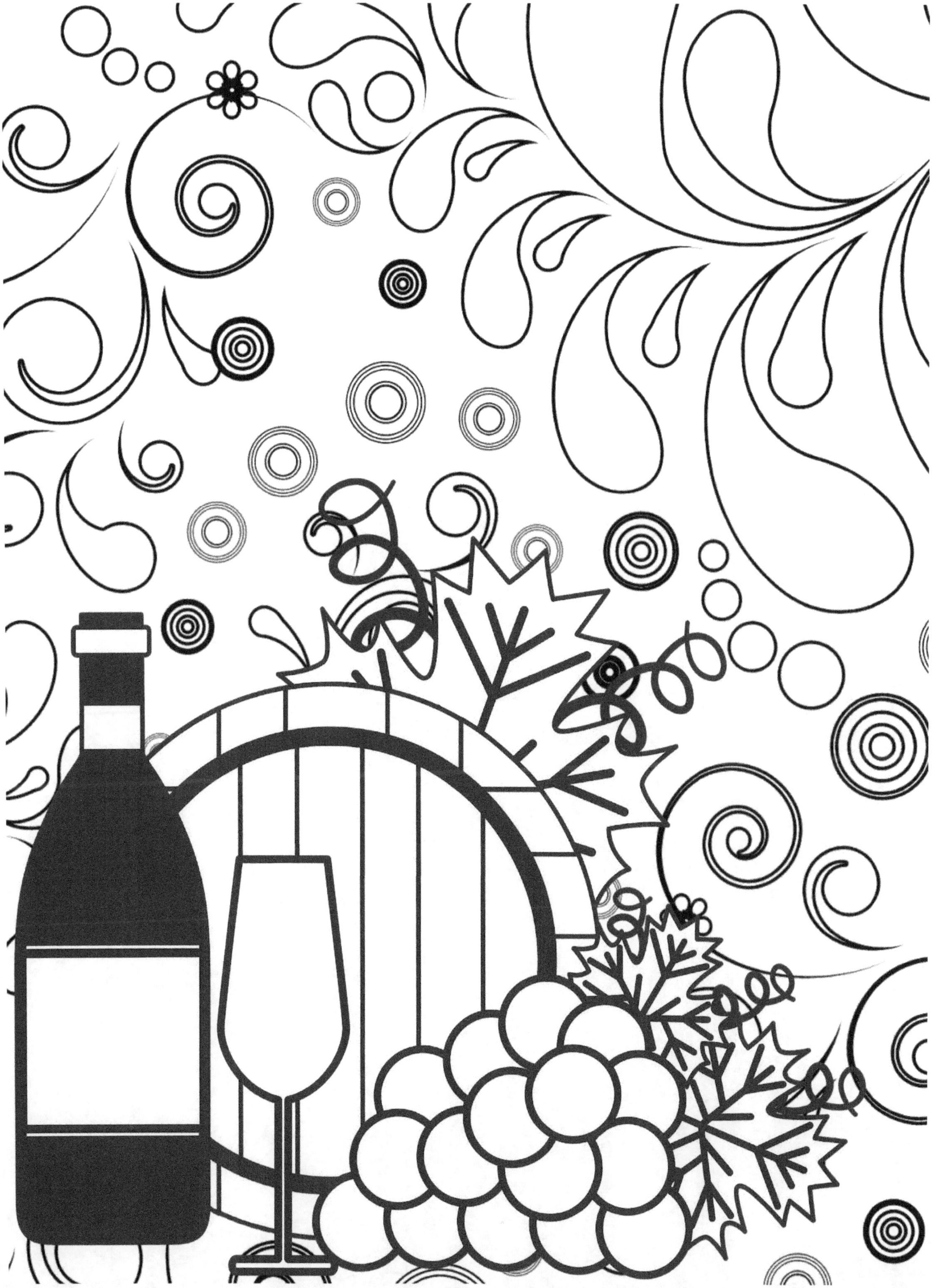

I Don't
Whine,
I Wine.

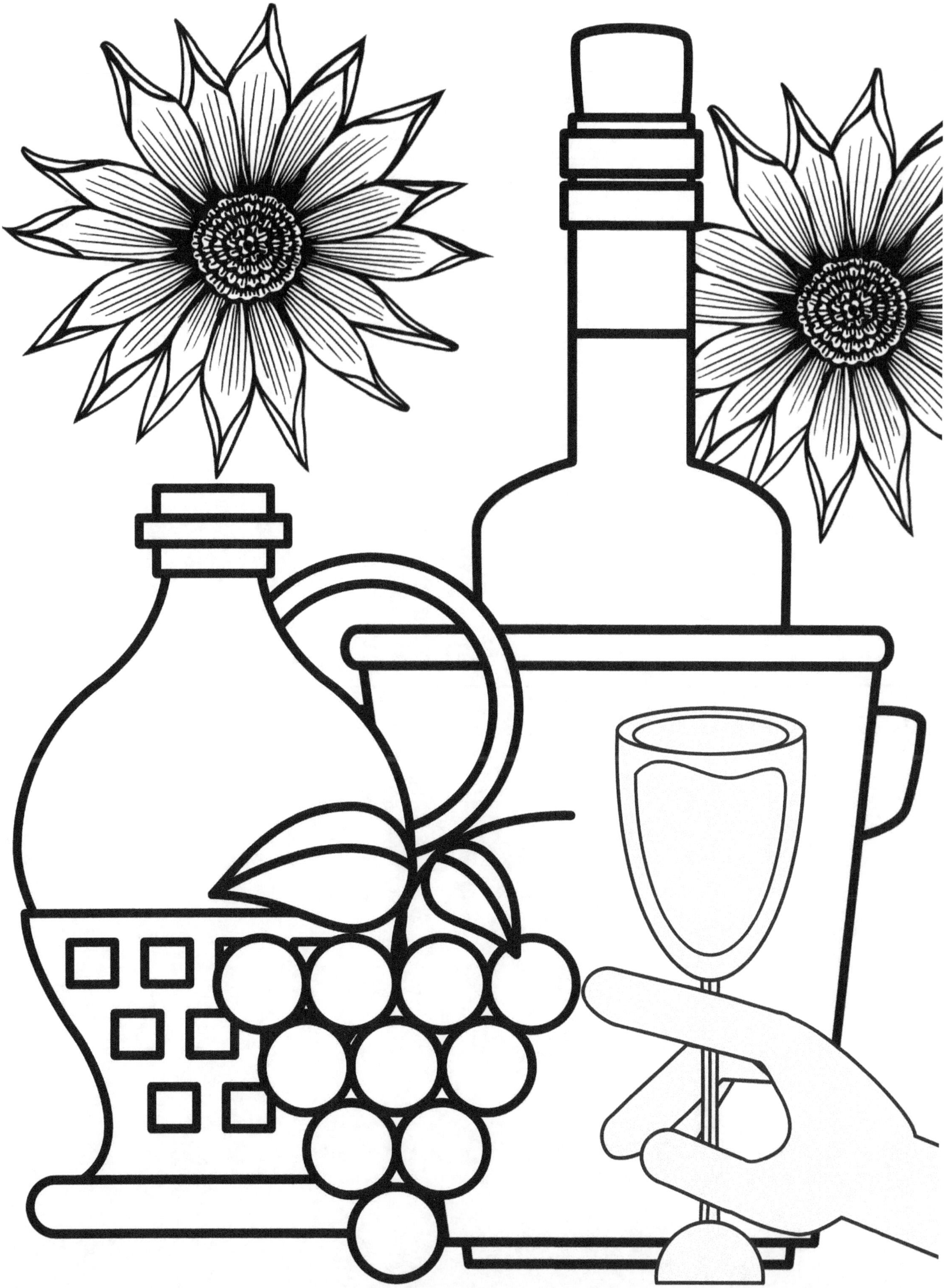

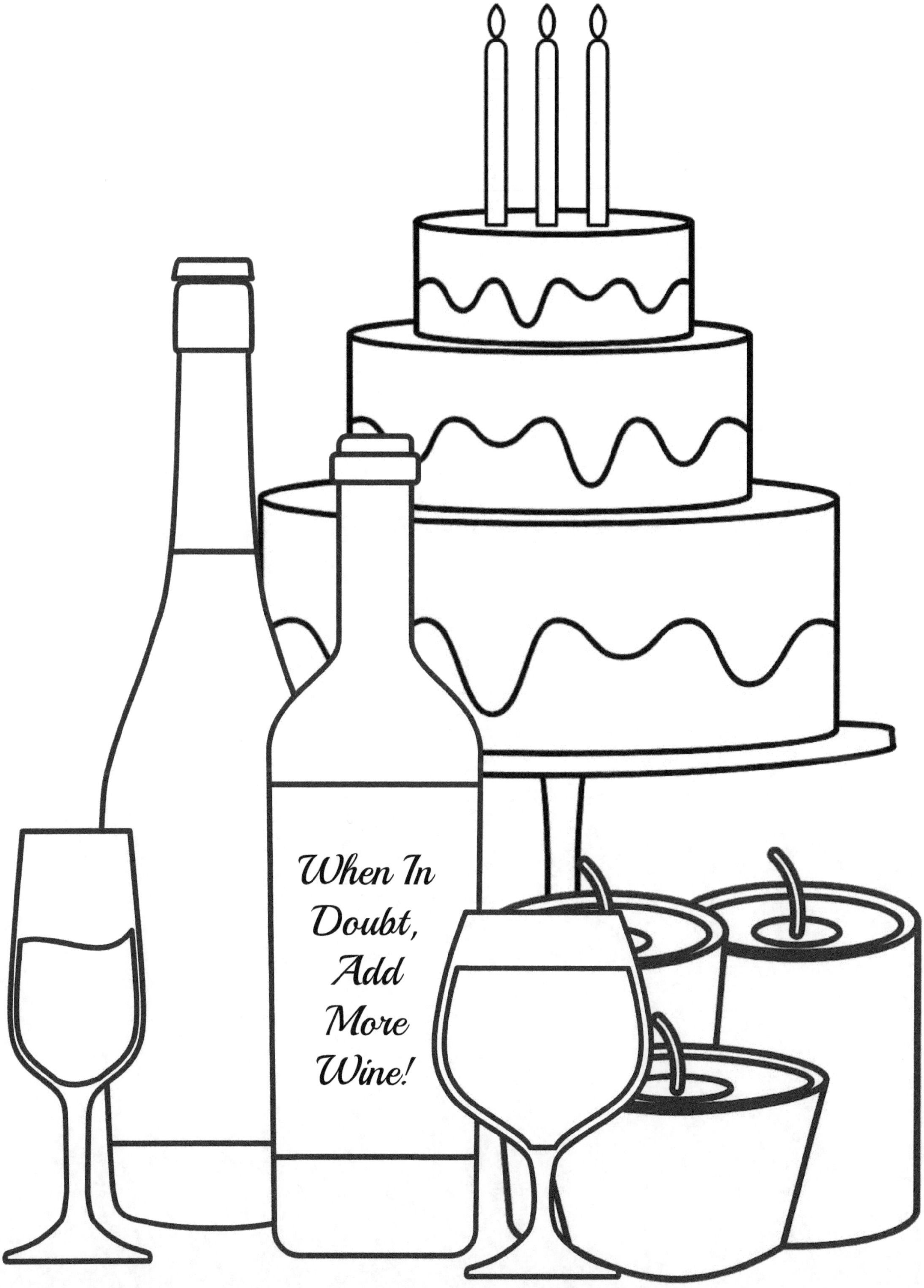
When In
Doubt,
Add
More
Wine!

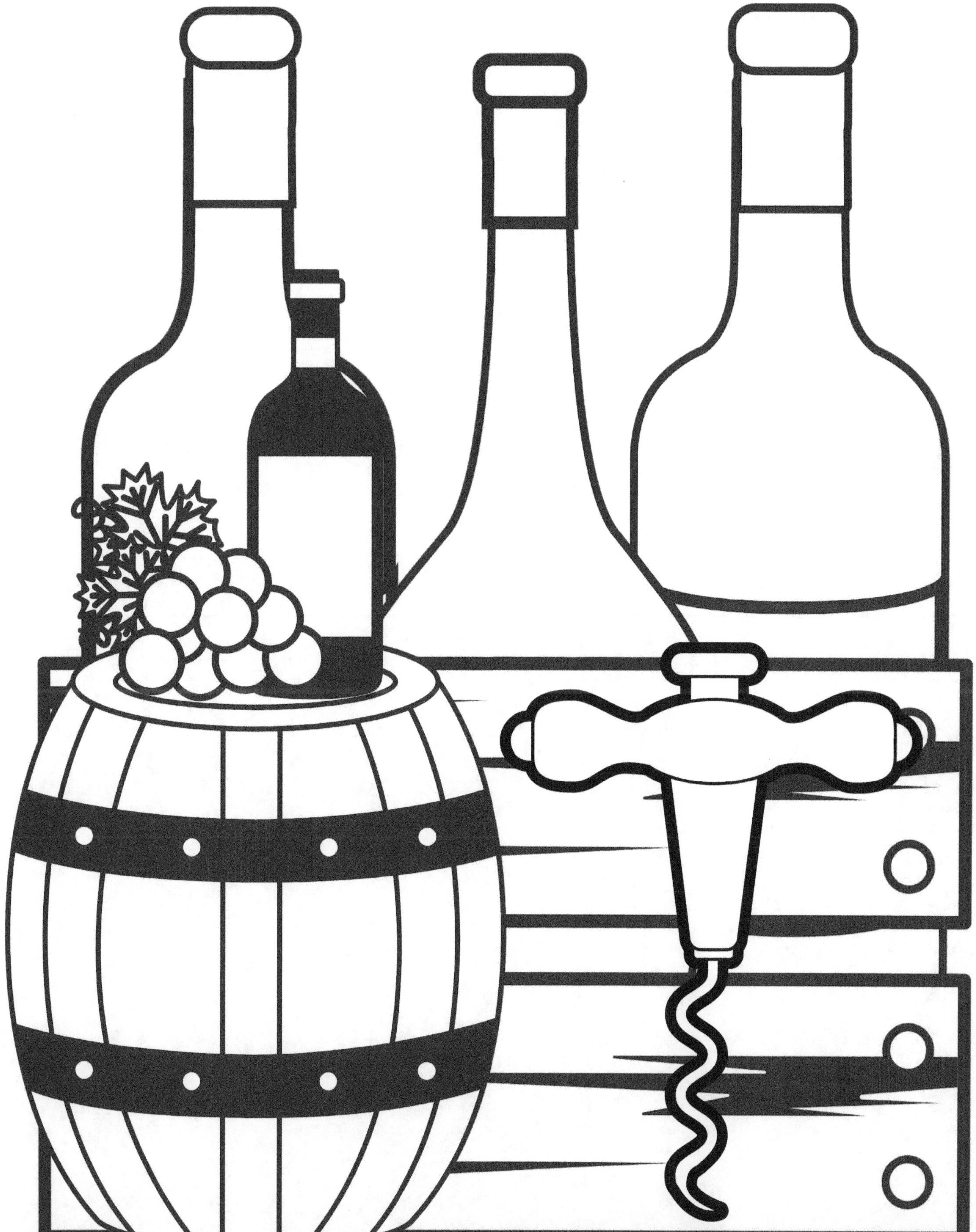

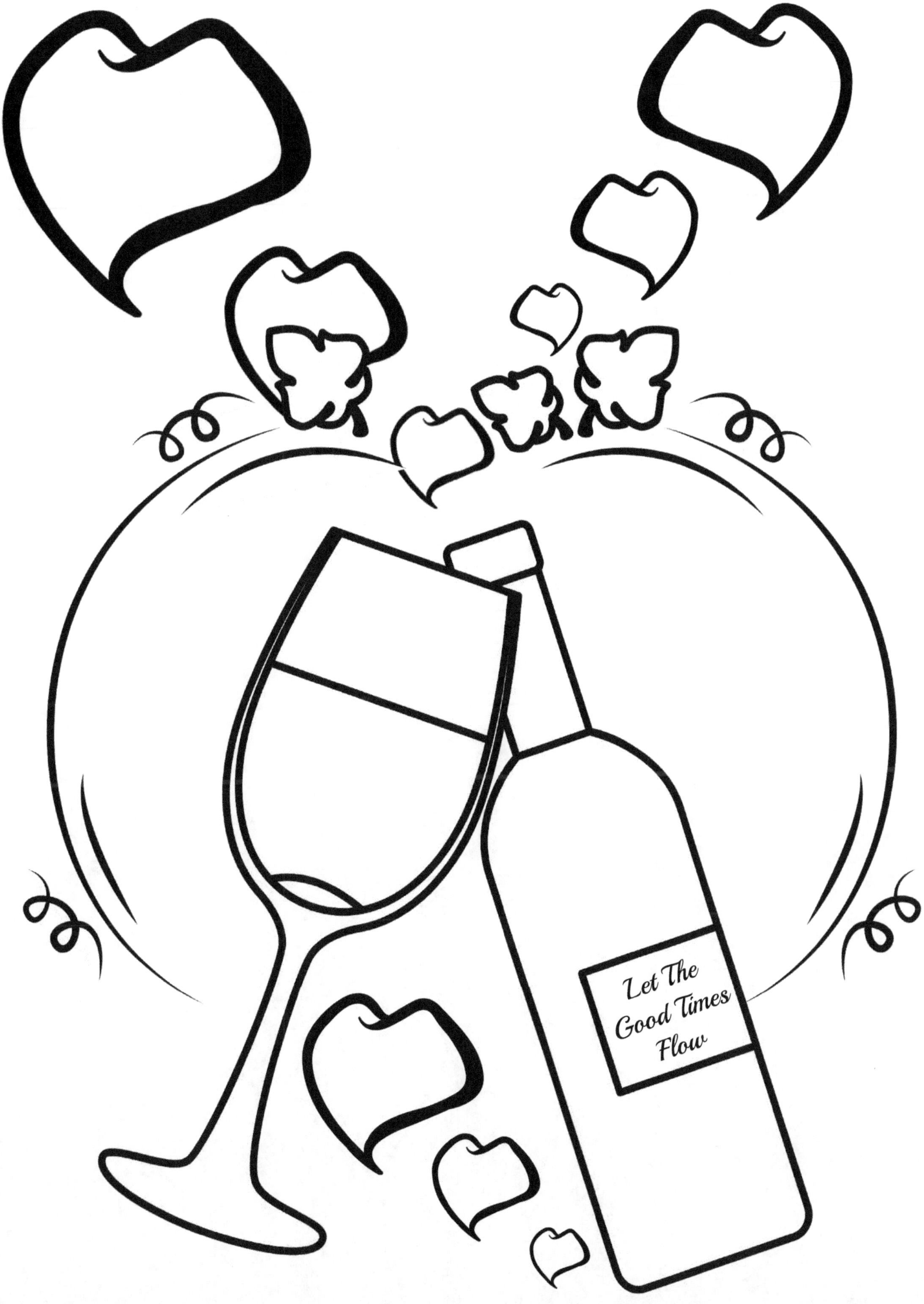
Let The
Good Times
Flow

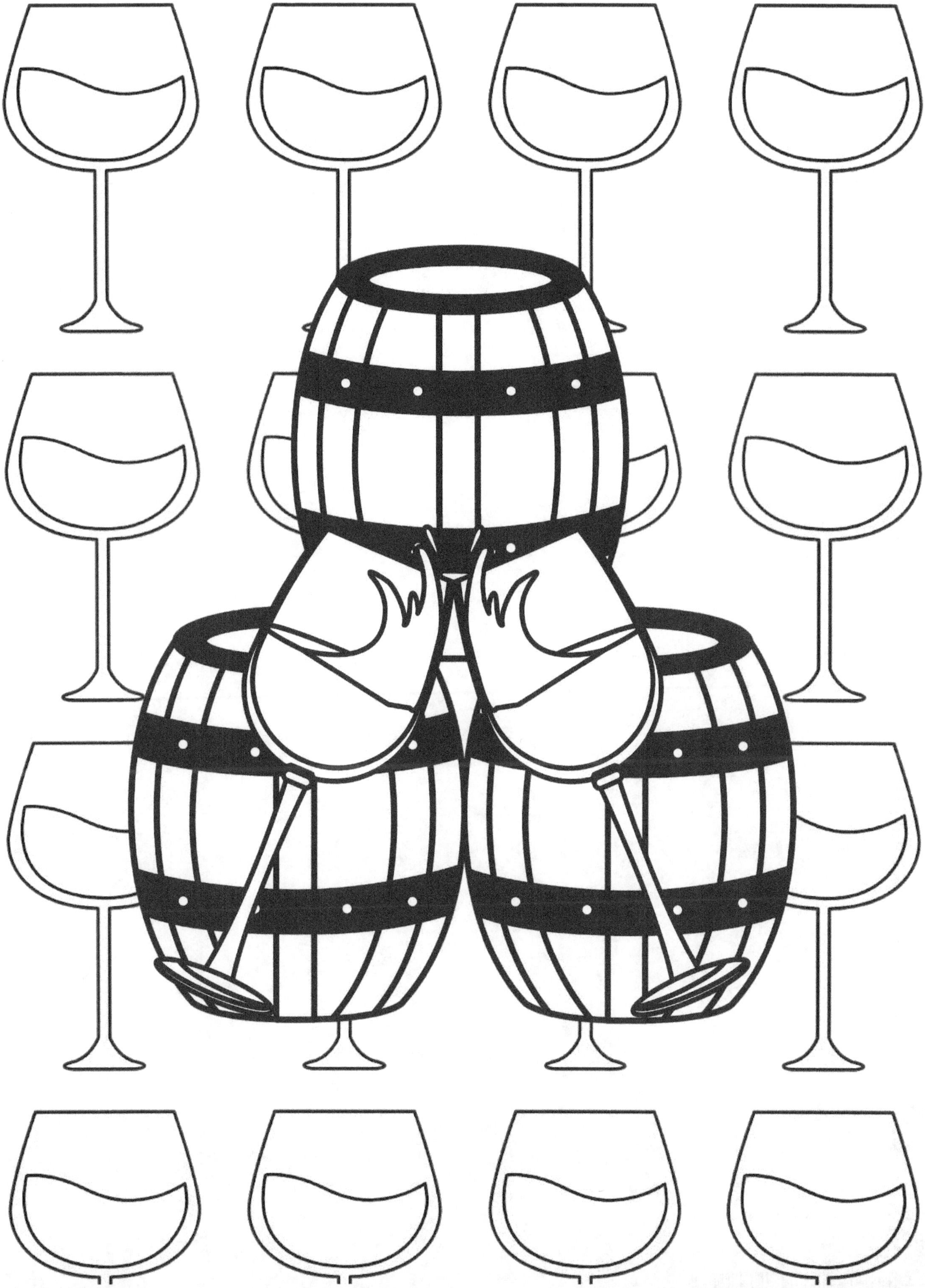

www.ingramcontent.com/pod-product-compliance
Lightning Source LLC
Chambersburg PA
CBHW080813170726
48000CB00020B/2995